Arthur Isaac Fonda

Honest Money

Arthur Isaac Fonda

Honest Money

ISBN/EAN: 9783744733816

Printed in Europe, USA, Canada, Australia, Japan

Cover: Foto ©ninafisch / pixelio.de

More available books at **www.hansebooks.com**

HONEST MONEY

BY

ARTHUR I. FONDA

New York
MACMILLAN AND CO.
AND LONDON
1895

All rights reserved

COPYRIGHT, 1895,
BY MACMILLAN AND CO.

Norwood Press:
J. S. Cushing & Co. — Berwick & Smith.
Norwood, Mass., U.S.A.

PREFACE.

In an article in the "American Journal of Politics" for July, 1893, I gave a brief statement of the conclusions I had reached in an attempt to analyze the requirements of a perfect money.

The limits of a magazine article prevented a full discussion of the subject; many points were left untouched, and all quotations from the works of other writers, in support of the brief arguments given, were of necessity omitted.

As the course of events since the article referred to was written has more fully confirmed the conclusions stated therein, a desire to give the subject ampler treatment, which its importance seems to demand, has led to the writing of this little work.

If apology is needed for a further contribution to the mass of literature on the subject of money, with which the country has of late been flooded, it must be found in the above explanation of the reasons which have led to the production of the present volume, coupled with the fact that the questions involved are far from being settled, and that the loud complaints, and the many financial schemes and plans, that have appeared all over the country make it probable that further legislation on the subject will be attempted in the near future.

It must be conceded that there is something radically wrong in a country like the United States, rich in all of the necessaries and most of the luxuries of life, where nature has been most bounteous, and where the not excessive population is exceptionally enterprising and industrious, when a large part of the people cannot at times find employment. When, with an abundance of unoccupied land, and a great diversity of undeveloped resources, capital and labor — both anxious for profitable employment — cannot find it; and when men suffer for the necessaries of life, not in one section only, but universally and in large numbers, while our warehouses are filled with manufactured goods, and our barns and granaries are bursting with food products. This is a condition that is certainly as wrong as it is unnecessary.

Such a condition occurring once or twice in the history of a country might be attributed to accident, but recurring, as it does, periodically, it argues a fault in our economic system. So wide a disturbance, extended also to other countries, betokens a general cause. What that cause is, it is not difficult to perceive — all indications point to our monetary system as the chief source of the trouble. There are doubtless other causes that contribute in some degree to create variations in prosperity, but no other single cause, or combination of causes, seems to us competent to account for the great fluctuations;

while the one we have cited alone may easily do so.

This work may have little direct effect in bringing about an improvement in our money system, but it is the hope of the writer that it may have at least an indirect effect by helping to spread a better knowledge of the requirements of such a system and of the principles involved.

Much of the current discussion of the subject of money betrays ignorance of those fundamental principles of the science which are agreed upon by all economists, if it does not wholly disregard them. I have endeavoured in this work to avoid such errors by a painstaking analysis of the subject, and by a careful comparison of the opinions of authorities on the principles involved. Starting from this foundation I have deduced the requirements for an honest money, shown the faults of our present system in the light of these requirements, as well as the merits and defects of various changes that have been proposed for its betterment, and, in conclusion, have outlined a system that seems to meet the requirements and to correct existing faults.

I desire to acknowledge my indebtedness, not only to the many works mentioned and quoted from herein, but to others, neither mentioned nor quoted, which have been of material assistance in corroborating the opinions I have ventured to advance.

A. I. F.

Denver, Colo.

CONTENTS.

CHAPTER I.

	PAGE
VALUE AND THE STANDARD OF VALUE	1
Definition of Value	1
Supply and Demand	8
The Standard of Value	12

CHAPTER II.

MONEY	21
Definition of Money	21
The Functions and Requirements of Money	25
Money Value	29
Money Demand and Supply	36
Necessity for Invariable Money Value	40

CHAPTER III.

EXISTING MONETARY SYSTEMS	51
The Gold Standard	54
Gresham's Law	57
The Silver Standard	65
Bi-metallism	67
Paper Money	71

CONTENTS.

CHAPTER IV.

	PAGE
STABILITY OF GOLD AND SILVER VALUES	81
Gold-Standard Prices	81
Silver-Standard Prices	94

CHAPTER V.

CRITICISM OF SOME GOLD-STANDARD ARGUMENTS	98

CHAPTER VI.

FOREIGN COMMERCE	112

CHAPTER VII.

MONEY IN THE UNITED STATES	125

CHAPTER VIII.

SOME PROPOSED CHANGES IN OUR MONEY SYSTEM	137

CHAPTER IX.

A NEW MONETARY SYSTEM	151
The Standard of Value	158
The Medium of Exchange	164

CHAPTER X.

MERITS AND OBJECTIONS CONSIDERED	181
Merits of Plan	181
Objections Answered	187

CHAPTER XI.

CONCLUSION	196
INDEX	205

HONEST MONEY.

CHAPTER I.

VALUE AND THE STANDARD OF VALUE.

Definition of Value.

A CLEAR conception of the meaning of the term *value* is the first essential to a discussion of the subject of money.

Under the general term *value* the older economists recognized two distinct conceptions, which they distinguished as *value in use* and *value in exchange*.

To the former they gave little attention, merely stating that while it was essential to value in exchange, the latter was not proportional to nor determined by the former, and citing air and water as familiar examples of objects having great utility, or use value, yet having little or no exchange value.

Modern economists — chiefly those of the Austrian school — have analyzed the subject more thoroughly, especially the relation between the two conceptions, and have shown that utility or subjective value, as it is generally termed by them, is an expression both of human desire and of the quantity of the necessary commodity available to satisfy such desire.

The utility of a thing grows less as the quantity of it increases, and it is the utility of the last increment of supply, or the marginal utility, that determines the subjective value of the whole supply, and it is the ratios between these subjective values that determine exchange values. Air and water, for instance, have no great utility, as viewed by the older economists, except where the supply is limited; ordinarily, their abundance makes their utility, or use value, small.

It is not essential to the purpose of this

work to enter into an abstract discussion of the theory of value further than is necessary to make clear the fact that the present analysis in no way lessens or invalidates the distinction between the two conceptions of value noted by the earlier economists, — a fact which has been overlooked by some who have accepted the marginal utility theory. The distinction remains, broad and clear. The one conception, whether called "value in use," "marginal utility," or "subjective value," pertains wholly to the relation which a single good, or unit group of goods, bears to a single individual, or society unit, in respect to human well-being, and has no reference or relation to any other individual or other good.

The other conception, called "objective value," or "exchange value," is dual in its nature, involving in all cases two or more commodities. Abstractly, it is *the ratio at which commodities may be exchanged for each other*, or, since such ratio for a unit of one commodity is expressed by the amount of another given for it, the exchange value of a thing is the quantity of some other thing that will be evenly exchanged for it, or, considered in a general sense, the amount of commodities in general it will exchange for, — *its general purchasing power*, in short.

This latter conception — exchange value — is the one that principally concerns us in discussing the subject of money. It is also the conception generally in mind when the simple term *value* is used either by economists or by the general public, and wherever the term is used in this work without qualification it is to be understood in that sense.

The Austrian economist, E. von Böhm-Bawerk, says, in his "Positive Theory of Capital," p. 130: —

"Value in the subjective sense is the importance which a good, or a complex of goods, possesses with regard to the well-being of a subject."

VALUE AND THE STANDARD OF VALUE. 5

"Besides the expression 'value in exchange,' English economists use, quite indifferently, the expression 'purchasing power,' and we Germans are beginning in the same way to put in general use the term *Tauschkraft.*"

The value of a thing may be considered either in a particular sense, with reference to some other specified thing, or it may be considered in a general sense, with reference to all other things considered as a whole. We may say the value of a bushel of wheat is two bushels of corn, meaning that these two commodities exchange for each other in that ratio; or we may speak of the value of wheat having risen or fallen, meaning that its general purchasing power, or the ratio between that and all other things taken as a unit or a whole, has increased or decreased.

The term must invariably be used or considered in a general sense, unless otherwise specifically stated, for we must always have some other thing in mind besides the one whose value we are considering; while if no other is stated, commodities in general (taken as a whole) is that thing.

Value being a ratio, it is impossible for all values to rise or fall simultaneously. The sum of subjective values may increase or decrease. — indeed it is one of the great objects of human endeavour to increase the sum of want-satisfying power, — but the sum of the ratios between these subjective values is constant. As one term of any ratio rises relative to the other, the second necessarily falls as regards the first.

This principle is so universally recognized that quotations might be given from almost every work on political economy in support of it. The following will be sufficient, however, as regards both the definition of value and this principle.

John Stuart Mill says, in his "Principles of Political Economy": —

"Value is a relative term. The value of a thing means the quantity of some other thing, or of things in general, which it exchanges for. The values of all things can never, therefore, rise or fall simultaneously. There is no such thing as a general rise or a general fall of values. Every rise of value supposes a fall, and every fall a rise."

Again, he says: —

"Things which are exchanged for one another can no more all fall, or all rise, than a dozen runners can each outstrip all the rest, or a hundred trees all overtop one another."

Prof. S. N. Patten says, in "Dynamic Economics," p. 64: "Objective values, however, are never a sum, but only a relation between subjective values. There can never be high or low objective values of commodities as a whole. It is therefore impossible to add to or subtract from them."

This latter quotation, as well as the preceding one from von Böhm-Bawerk, — both exponents of the marginal utility theory, — may help to correct a quite prevalent impression that this later theory does not distinguish between the two conceptions of value, and that because the sum of subjective values may increase, the sum of objective or exchange values can increase also.

Supply and Demand.

All economists recognize the fact that the immediate determiner of value is the relation between supply and demand. These terms in their economic sense mean something more than mere desire and mere quantity. *Supply* means the amount offered in exchange, and *demand* means not only a desire, but a desire coupled with the ability and willingness to give other commodities in exchange for the one wanted.

In this sense the terms are strictly correlative. The supply of a commodity (that is, the amount offered) may be considered as equivalent to a demand for some other commodity, or for commodities in general. We may say, then, that the value of any commodity is determined by the ratio that the demand for that commodity bears to its supply; or by the ratio that the demand for that commodity bears to the demand for some other commodity,—or commodities in general, when the term *value* is used in a general sense and not with reference to some other specified thing only. (The objection that has been made by some writers that a ratio could not logically exist between a desire [demand] and a quantity [supply], does not apply to these terms in their economic sense ; for, as above stated, they are something more than a mere desire and a mere quantity, and the expression is translatable into the other expression, " ratio between the demand for one commodity and the demand for others in general.")

The statement of the later economists that exchange value depends on, and is determined by, the ratio between subjective values in no way conflicts with the above statement that value is determined by the ratio between demand and supply, for the demand for a commodity is determined by its subjective value and by that alone, and must vary with it. Hence, as the quantity of anything increases and its subjective value lessens, the demand for it relative to the quantity of other articles also lessens, and its value falls, and *vice versa*.

This close connection between value and the ratio between demand and supply — value rising as the ratio increases, and falling as it grows less — is true in all cases. No other factor can affect the value of any commodity except by altering the relation or ratio between these two.

Cost of production is a more remote factor that enters into the determination of value in most but not in all cases, through its effect on supply. It is used, like the term *value*, in two senses, a subjective and an objective sense. In the former it means the pain of labour and waiting that must be undergone to produce the good that is being considered, — the negative pleasure given to get the positive pleasure to be derived from that good. In its objective sense — the sense in which it is generally used — cost of production means the goods that must otherwise be given for, bartered or set against those desired; in a simple case of direct production, it means the goods that might have been produced, in lieu of those that have been produced, with the same subjective cost; in more complex cases, it means the sum of the goods sacrificed, in the shape of raw materials, rent, wages, interest, etc., to get the one produced.

When the value of a commodity falls to or below the cost of production, or even when it approaches it so closely as to reduce the margin between the two — the producer's profit — below that in other industries, then, men will cease to produce the one and turn their labour and capital to producing the others which offer greater profit, thus lowering the supply of the abandoned product and raising that of the more profitable, thereby affecting the value of both.

The effect of this operation of the law of

cost is to equalize profits and make the values of things conform to their cost or be proportional thereto.

The law can only operate when men are free to turn their labour from one industry to another. Hence arises the important exception to the law, that the values of goods produced by a monopoly are not affected by their cost of production. Only under free competition does the law operate in full force. As monopoly becomes a factor cost ceases to be, and, when the monopoly is complete, cost has no weight whatever in the determination of value.

For analogous reasons, cost enters but partially into the determination of the value of such goods as are dependent more or less on luck or chance for their production, as in the case of precious stones, gold, silver, etc.

The Standard of Value.

We may use the value of anything as a measure by which to compare the values of any and all other things. but as all the factors that determine value are variable, the value of everything is variable. Any value may rise with reference to some other value, and at the same time fall with reference to a third.

By what standard, or invariable measure at all times and places, can we compare the values of goods to determine their constancy or variability?

We must not forget that there are two kinds of value, and that it is a standard of exchange value we are seeking. So far as it may be possible to formulate a standard of subjective value, it must consist of the pain or inutility of labour; for this kind of value pertains only to a single good, and cannot be referred to other goods without confusing it with the other conception. We cannot measure the absolute pleasure a good will give to an individual except by the pain he will undergo to get it. It is not a standard for this sort of value we want. It was evidently some such conception as the above — confusing, however, not only the two kinds of value but the two descriptions of labour — that led Adam Smith to consider labour as the ultimate standard of value. He appears also to have confused the idea of a standard of value with that of a determiner of value.

These errors were pointed out in part by Ricardo and, in part also, by J. S. Mill and later writers; hence the contention that labour is in any way a standard of value has long been abandoned by the ablest economists. The idea still lingers, however, and is frequently brought forward in current discussions, and for this reason it seems necessary to analyze briefly the relation of labour to value.

Labour is necessary to the production of all commodities, but it is not itself a commodity, nor anything which for itself is desired. It is a force, and, like every force, valuable according to the results it accomplishes. If unproductive, it has no value; if productive, its value varies according to the value of the commodities or utilities it creates. We use the terms "price of labour" or "value of labour," implying that it is the labour which is valued, and which is bought and sold; but the terms are merely a convenience. What is really bought and sold is the commodity or utility such labour has produced or will produce. If it were the labour itself, then the purchaser would receive not only the labour, but the commodity it produced, in exchange for the wages paid,—a double return,—which, of course, is absurd.

Three descriptions of labour may be distinguished in connection with the value of a commodity, viz.:—

(1) The labour expended in its production.

(2) The labour in general it will purchase.

(3) The labour necessary to produce more of it.

The first kind of labour in no way affects the existing supply or demand of the commodity, and is neither a measure of its value nor a regulator or determining factor of such value. Evidences are not lacking to prove that a commodity will frequently not exchange for as much labour as was expended in producing it.

The second kind of labour, the amount in general which a commodity will purchase, depends on the amount of commodities such labour will produce, less the share which goes to capital as its reward; for, neglecting rent or classing it with capital, these two, labour and capital, are joint factors in production and divide between them the total product. It is hardly necessary to observe that labour is continually growing more efficient; that improved skill and methods enable a much larger amount of commodities in general to be produced, with a certain amount of labour, than could formerly be produced; and that labour receives, as its share of such product, a much larger amount than formerly.

It is thus evident, that a commodity which would exchange for the same amount of labour now as formerly, would exchange for a much larger amount of commodities in general now than then, and, if we adhere to our definition of exchange value, would be worth *more* than formerly; while if labour be taken as a standard of value, it would be worth the *same*. The use of this form of labour as a standard of value is, it will be seen, incompatible with the definition of value. It may serve as a measure of the relative values of two commodities at any particular time and place, just as any third commodity may; but, as Ricardo remarks, "is subject to as many fluctuations as the commodities compared with it."

The same argument applies to the third form of labour — that necessary to produce more of a commodity. This form of labour, however, is one of the factors in the cost of production, and through its effect on cost is one of the more remote factors that determine value, as explained in considering cost of production, but this does not make it in any sense a standard.

c

We may conclude, then, that labour in any form is not a standard of value; that, as John Stuart Mill observes, it "discards the idea of exchange value altogether, substituting a totally different idea, more analogous to value in use."

Since the values of things can never rise or fall simultaneously, every rise supposing a fall, and every fall a rise, it follows that the values of all taken together must be constant; in other words, that general values cannot change. Thus it is that we find whether any one thing has risen or fallen in value, as between one period and another, only by comparing it with all others, — in short, by its general exchange or purchasing power. If this has increased, then its value has risen; if it has decreased, its value has fallen. It is evidently not necessary that anything should exchange for more or less of *every* other thing to show a rise or fall of value, but only that it should, on the average, exchange for more or less of all; that its average purchasing power should be greater or less. If it has exchanged at different times for the same amounts, on the average, of all other things, its value, clearly, has remained constant.

This is the only standard, or test, which can be applied to the exchange value of any commodity to determine its constancy or variability, and it is inherent in the very definition of exchange value.

The values of commodities may be compared to the surface of the ocean, which, vexed by winds and tides, is never at rest, every point continually rising or falling as compared with others. As some points rise others fall, yet there is a mean level which does not vary, and by comparison with which the variations of level of any particular point may be determined. So with values, there is a mean or average which is constant, and by referring individual values to that we can determine their fluctuations.

These ideas will become clearer as we proceed to apply them concretely to the special case of money.

Although there can be but one real *standard of value,* invariable at all times and places, yet, as before stated, any commodity may serve as a *measure of value,* and the great convenience subserved, by all the people of any locality or country using the same commodity instead of a number of different ones for this purpose, early led to the adoption of some one commodity in each locality as a "money" to measure values and facilitate exchanges.

CHAPTER II.

MONEY.

Definition of Money.

Money has been variously defined by different writers. Perhaps the definition given by Prof. F. A. Walker, though lengthy, is the most comprehensive. He says: "Money is that which passes freely from hand to hand throughout the community in final discharge of debts and full payment for commodities, being accepted equally without reference to the character or credit of the person who offers it, and without the intention of the person who receives it to consume it, or enjoy it, or to apply it to any other use than in turn to tender it to others in discharge of debts or full payment for commodities."

This definition has been indorsed by several other writers; by some, however, the term *money* is restricted to coin, paper money being called currency. The distinction is perfectly proper, though not generally concurred in. People commonly use the terms *money* and *currency* indiscriminately for both coin and paper money, since they perform identically the same work where both are used together, and the paper is convertible into coin at any time. Where the paper is used alone — "inconvertible paper" — coin is really not money; it ceases to circulate as money; it is hoarded as treasure, or bought and sold as a commodity, but fails to have that general use in current transactions in that country which alone entitles any commodity to be called money.

The distinction sought to be made between paper money and coin arises largely, it is thought, from the idea that coin has a value in itself which paper money has not. This idea is erroneous. Value, as we have seen, is a ratio or relation, and though the value of anything is based on a desire for it, that desire may arise either from the satisfaction which the use or consumption of it will bring, or from the belief that it can be exchanged for some other thing that will give satisfaction in use or consumption. The value of money is due to the latter of these two causes. No one wants money except for the purpose of exchanging it for other commodities; under modern conditions it is necessary for this purpose, — it is the indispensable requisite to the satisfaction of certain human wants. Money, therefore, possesses an indirect if not a direct subjective value which forms the basis of its exchange value. Paper money possesses the power of satisfying this need for money to the same extent that coin does, under like conditions, and it has, therefore, both subjective value and exchange value, and the latter is governed by the same law of supply and demand that operates in all cases.

The fact that the material of which the money is made is, in one instance, of great cost, and, in the other, of little or no cost, is of minor consequence. The minting of gold and silver into coin may, or may not, add to its value; it really transforms it into another commodity — money — and its value is thenceforth determined by the law of supply and demand as applied to money. The same is true of paper money, the low cost in the production of which is not an element in determining its value, for its production is always a monopoly. There is no reason, then, for not considering paper currency as money, and in using the term we will consider its meaning to be that given by Professor Walker, — which is also its popular significance, — and as including both paper money and coin.

It should be considered, whether of one material or of several circulating concurrently, as a single commodity created for the purpose it fulfils, and as separate and distinct from the material of which it is made. In short, as that commodity to which, by common consent and usage, generally sanctioned by law, all other commodities are referred as a measure of value, and by means of which exchanges are effected.

The Functions and Requirements of Money.

Professor Jevons, in his valuable work, "Money and the Mechanism of Exchange," gives to money the following threefold functions, viz. as:—

A medium of exchange.

A measure of value.

A standard of deferred payments.

He also inquires if it does not perform a fourth function as a 'store of value.'

All authorities give the first two of the above as the principal money functions. Some include one or both of the others, and some omit both.

Prof. F. A. Walker objects to the use of the term "measure of value," on the ground that value, being a relation, cannot be measured but can only be expressed. He proposes, instead, the term, "common denominator of value." It is not quite clear why a relation or ratio cannot be measured,—the measure, of course, being a similar ratio,—nor does there seem to be anything gained by the change, while the term proposed seems less clear and correct than the one in general use. Money, or the *value* of the unit of money, is used as a measure in comparing the values of other things just as a yardstick, or the *length* of a yard, is used in comparing the lengths of other objects.

Money, in acting as a medium of exchange, must also act as a store of value to some extent, since it stores the value received until it is expended; but the use of money for the purpose of hoarding is not to be regarded as strictly one of its functions, at least not in the sense of requiring to be especially provided for. The fact that it is so used, however, should be borne in mind, as it interferes more or less with its other and more important functions; but in considering the qualities necessary to the best performance of the functions of money we may omit this last function, as any money which fills the requirements for the others will fulfil those necessary to this in a sufficient degree considering its minor importance. As our inquiries in this work will be confined to the money materials now in general use, viz., gold, silver, and paper, we need not consider the qualities necessary to a money material, as given by Professor Jevons,— such as portability, indestructibility, divisibility, etc.,— further than to say that the qualities he mentions are possessed by all of the money materials now in use, in a sufficient and nearly equal degree. Coin, to be sure, is more indestructible than paper; but as the paper is sufficiently acceptable for the purpose, the difference need not concern us.

Aside from that general acceptability, which is the very essence of money,— without which no commodity could be considered money, and which, therefore, all money may be considered as having, — the great requirements of money are *invariable value*, added to *convenience of form, size, weight, and value.*

This latter requirement pertains to the function of a medium of exchange, and the degree in which it is possessed by the different money materials or kinds of money, depends wholly on the values to be transferred by its use. For small amounts, silver is preferable to either gold or paper; as the amount increases, gold becomes preferable to silver; and for all amounts above fractional currency, paper money is unquestionably more convenient in every way than either gold or silver, and the advantage increases with the amount.

Invariable value is the great requirement for both the functions, — "a measure of value" and "a standard of deferred payments." Indeed these two functions may practically be considered one; the only difference between them being centred in the element of time, and that is more or less involved in every exchange requiring the use of money, since some interval must elapse between the sale of one commodity and the purchase of another with the money received, — which constitutes the whole exchange transaction, — and during such interval the money should maintain a constant value. When the interval over which the transaction is spread is a large one, as in the case of notes and bonds, any variability is more noticeable than when the change is distributed among many holders of money.

Before considering further the great necessity for invariable money value, it will be best to consider the laws and forces which determine and control the value of money.

Money Value.

That money is a commodity, and that its value varies like that of every commodity in accordance with the law of supply and demand, are incontestable.

The fluctuations in the value of money can be detected, it is clear, in the same way that changes in the value of any commodity can be detected, by comparison with all other commodities. — by its average purchasing power, in short.

The value of a commodity, when measured by money and expressed in terms of the unit of money, is called its *price*. If the prices of all commodities, or the average of all, rise or fall, it is conclusive evidence that the value of money has changed, for its purchasing power is less in the one case and greater in the other. Indeed the statement that general prices have fallen is equivalent to saying that the value of money has increased, and *vice versa*. Therefore, if the value of money remains stable, average prices must remain constant.

The following quotations will show that these views are correct, and that they are generally accepted by authorities on finance and political economy, though very commonly overlooked and neglected in discussions on the subject.

John Stuart Mill, in his "Principles of Political Economy," says:—

"There is such a thing as a general rise of prices. All commodities may rise in their money price. But there cannot be a general rise of values. It is a contradiction in terms." "That the money prices of all things should rise or fall, provided all rise or fall equally, is in itself, and apart from existing contracts, of no consequence. It affects nobody's wages, profits, or rent. Every one gets more money in the one case and less in the other; but of all that is to be bought with money they get neither more nor less than before. It makes no other difference than that of using more or fewer counters to reckon by. The only thing which in this case is really altered in value is money; and the only persons who either gain or lose are the holders of money, or those who have to receive or pay fixed sums of it. . . . There is a disturbance, in short, of fixed money contracts, and this is an evil whether it takes place in the debtor's favour or in the creditor's. . . . Let it therefore be remembered (and occasions will often rise for calling it to mind) that a general rise or a general fall of values is a contradiction; and that a general rise of prices is merely tantamount to an alteration in the value of money, and is a matter of complete indifference save in so far as it affects existing contracts for receiving and paying fixed pecuniary amounts."

"The value of a thing is what it will exchange for: the value of money is what money will exchange for; the purchasing power of money. If prices are low, money will buy much of other things, and is of high value; if prices are high, it will buy little of other things, and is of low value. The value of money is inversely as general prices: falling as they rise and rising as they fall."

"The value of money, other things being

the same, varies inversely as its quantity; every increase of quantity lowering the value, and every diminution raising it in a ratio exactly equivalent."

"That an increase of the quantity of money raises prices, and a diminution lowers them, is the most elementary proposition in the theory of currency."

The expression, "other things being the same," in one of these quotations, evidently means "demand remaining the same," and the terms *increase* and *decrease* of money unquestionably refer to the increase and decrease relative to demand, since the writer further says: —

"If there be at any time an increase in the number of money transactions, a thing continually liable to happen from differences in the activity of speculation, and even in the time of year (since certain kinds of business are transacted only at particular seasons); an increase of the currency which is only proportional to this increase of transactions, and is of no longer duration, has no tendency to raise prices."

Per contra, therefore, unless the currency be increased to meet such increased demand, there will be a tendency to decreased prices and consequent change in the value of money.

Stronger statements than these of Mill's, or by an abler authority, could not be asked for.

Prof. R. T. Ely, in his " Political Economy," remarks, p. 179: —

" Values are merely relative, and consequently there can be no such thing as a general rise or fall of values."

" Value expressed in money is called price. There can be such a thing as a general fall or a general rise of prices. A general fall in prices means an increase in the value of money, and a general rise of prices means a fall in the value of money."

David Ricardo observes that: —

" The value of money, then, does not wholly depend upon its absolute quantity.

but on its quantity relatively to the payments it has to accomplish."

The last edition of the "Encyclopædia Britannica" says, as a conclusion in discussing the value of money, and referring evidently to coin alone: —

"The most correct way to regard the question of money value is that which looks on supply and demand, as interpreted above, as the regulator of its value for a limited time, while regarding cost of production as a force exercising an influence of uncertain amount on its fluctuations during long periods."

This view is in exact accordance with the conclusions previously stated in regard to the values of all commodities.

The Encyclopædia further says: —

"Where the coinage of a State is artificially limited, the value of its money plainly depends on supply and demand."

Quotations might be multiplied indefinitely to the same effect; but enough have been given to show the general consensus of opinion.

Indeed it may seem that there is no necessity for accumulating evidence in support of propositions so apparent as those stated; unfortunately, however, not a few recent writers have ignored some of them, and the general public seem to make the same mistake; hence, it is of the utmost importance that they be kept clearly in mind.

Money Demand and Supply.

Mill affirms that: "The supply of money is all the money *in circulation* at the time."

Money that is hoarded has no more effect on prices than if it did not exist. Money lying in banks or in the hands of merchants or others to the extent necessary for the safe conduct of their business may be considered money in circulation, but beyond the amount needed for conducting any business the excess may be considered as hoarded. The supply of money in any country depends directly and primarily on the legislation of that country; and secondarily, in most, but not in all cases, on the legislation of other countries, and the production of precious metals available for coinage, etc., all of which can be better analyzed in explaining the different systems.

The demand for money is most complicated, since it is affected by a great variety of forces. It varies directly with the activity of commerce, and universally with the activity of money, — a less amount of money doing a greater work when active than when sluggish. It is affected by changes in the customs and habits of the people, by changes in transportation facilities, in diversity of employment, in concentration of population, and, more than all other, it is affected by the extent of credit, the use of banking facilities, etc.

Credit in its various forms takes the place of money, and does its work in this respect to an enormous and continually increasing extent. Through the medium of banks, — which are really institutions for the exchange of credit, — and by means of checks, drafts, notes, bills of exchange, letters of credit, post-office and express money orders, etc., the great bulk of the world's business is transacted.

Statistics gathered from national banks in this country in 1881, showed that of the total deposits, ninety-five (95) per cent were in forms of credit to five (5) per cent in actual money, the percentage of credit paper rising in New York City to as high as 98.7.

While these percentages may not show accurately, on the whole, the relative work done by money and by forms of credit, they do show the enormous extent to which credit takes the place of money, and the greatly increased demand for money that arises, when, from lack of confidence or other causes, the extent of the credit is lessened. Unless the volume of money immediately adapts itself to such demand, the value of money must inevitably increase, or the demand be lessened by a checking of all business transactions, and a partial paralysis of the industries of the country. Generally both of these results follow.

With these facts in mind, it is evidently futile to attempt to fix any definite amount of money, per capita, as the proper one. Not only does the amount necessary to meet the demand vary with different countries, per capita, even among the most civilized nations, but it varies with the seasons in each country, as crops have to be moved or not, and with the state of credit and enterprise from day to day. France, where the habits and customs of the people have prevented their making so large a use of credit and banking facilities as in England, requires a larger amount of money, per capita, than does England.

Since the value of money depends on these two factors, supply and demand, if we are to have a money of invariable value, we must evidently control one or both of these. It would be hopeless to attempt to control all the various conditions and forces which, we have seen, affect the demand for money. Fortunately it is not necessary. We cannot control the demand, but we have, or can have, complete control over the supply, and we can by this means maintain that constant relation between the supply of, and the demand for, money which is essential to its stability of value.

Necessity for Invariable Money Value.

Returning to the reasons for an invariable money value, they are best appreciated by considering the effects of one that is variable. While the statement of Mill, previously quoted, "that the money prices of all things should rise or fall, provided all rise or fall equally, is in itself and apart from existing contracts, of no consequence," is true, yet is it true only under the condition specified, that *all shall rise or fall equally*, and this condition in the case of a fluctuating money value never obtains. Aside from the exception which Mill makes of fixed money contracts, which can never adjust themselves at all to a changed money value, — and the exception is of enormous volume and importance, — the prices of many commodities are not adjustable quickly or readily to a change in money value, especially when such change is an increase. There is a persistency or inertia about prices that in many instances resists a reduction. Wages can never be reduced without friction and often strikes. The fact that commodities have fallen and that the lower wages will buy as much, or more, than the higher ones formerly did, is slow of appreciation: hence the employer caught between the difficulty of reducing his employés' wages and the falling prices of his products, is injured by an increased money value. When the change, on the other hand, is a decrease of money value, the employer will not as a rule advance wages until compelled to do so, and the labourer suffers meanwhile from the rising prices of commodities.

When prices fall, the producers of a commodity are not apt to recognize that it is a general fall, a change in money value; but accustomed to regard money as invariable in value, as it should be, and, failing to see anything in the conditions affecting their own particular product that should lower the price, they delay or refuse to sell, hoping for higher prices; and all, or a large number, doing this, makes business dull.

The great injury and evil of changing money value comes, however, through fixed money contracts. The enormous amount of bonded indebtedness, railroad, municipal, county, state, and national, makes the slightest change of money value of vast importance, and added to these is the aggregate volume of commercial and private debts.

In short, a change of money value either way is a robbery, and none the less reprehensible because it is legal and insidious. Indeed, it is perhaps more damaging in its secondary effects because of its insidiousness. An open danger may be guarded against, but the hidden danger, known to exist, but which cannot be located or prevented, only excites fear and distrust, and checks all movement. Nor is the damage, in its secondary effects, confined to those involved in fixed money contracts. Piracy on the seas or robbery on a highway, when common, injure not alone those who are robbed. The fear and distrust engendered by such occurrences damage and delay all commerce; and the cost of protection against these menaces, or of avoiding them by taking more circuitous routes, are a burden on the whole people. So the robbery by a fluctuating money value affects, indirectly, the whole community, while the indirect effects are far worse. In the case of a decreasing money value the robbery does not bring such disastrous consequences in its train as where the change is an increase, owing to the different conditions of the people robbed.

A slight decrease of money value generally brings about a stimulation of trade and industry, the rising prices of commodities acting as a spur to greater production and new enterprises.

Mr. F. A. Walker, indeed, considers that for this reason, and in spite of the recognized injustice to some classes, that such a condition when slight and brought about by natural causes, is a benefit on the whole. It can hardly be admitted that robbery of one large class in a community is defensible, even if it does result in a gain to another class greater than the loss to the first. It is indisputable, however, that the opposite case, where money is increasing in value, brings such disasters in its train that it would be better, if an invariable value for money could not be attained, that the variation should be a decrease rather than an increase. In the latter case not only is the robbery equally great, but falling upon the most active, industrious, and enterprising class of the community, — for it is this class as a rule that are borrowers, — it not only imperils all they possess, but discourages, when long continued, all forms of industry and enterprise. In this way it throws thousands of men out of employment and brings suffering and hardship to thousands more. No other one cause, perhaps, is more responsible for "panics" and "hard times," with their attendant evils — tramps, pauperism, and crime. Its evils have been painted by many writers, and it is scarcely possible to exaggerate them. Of all ills, war and pestilence alone seem to fill the cup of human suffering more nearly full than the depression and stagnation of industry which is brought about by constantly declining prices.

In view of these facts, the necessity for a money that shall vary in its amount in accordance with the demands of business is evident. Not only must it respond to the long-continued, slow, and almost imperceptible increase of demand due to growing trade and population, but it should also respond, quickly and surely, to those sudden demands, known as panics, when credit fails for any reason to do its usual work. This need is recognized by bankers in their demand for a flexible or elastic currency.

Quotations are hardly necessary in support of the foregoing statements, but a few may be given. David Ricardo, in "Proposals for an Economic and Secure Currency," observes that: —

"All writers on the subject of money have agreed that uniformity in the value of the circulating medium is an object greatly to be desired."

"A currency may be considered as perfect of which the standard is invariable, which always conforms to that standard, and in the use of which the utmost economy is practised."

"During the late discussions on the bullion question, it was most justly contended, that a currency to be perfect should be absolutely invariable in value."

Prof. J. L. Laughlin, in "The History of Bi-metallism in the United States," remarks, p. 70: —

"The highest justice is rendered by the state when it exacts from the debtor at the end of a contract the *same purchasing power* which the creditor gave him at the beginning of the contract, no less, no more."

Prof. R. T. Ely says, in his "Political Economy," p. 191: —

"It is not the 'much or little,' but it is the 'more or less' that is of vital concern. Nothing produces more intense suffering than a decrease in the amount of money, and this is on account of the connection between past, present, and future in our economic life."

This refers to a decrease relative to the demand, evidently, and he says, further: —

"If the amount of money is arbitrarily increased, so that the value of all debts may fall, it amounts to virtual robbery of the creditors. When arbitrarily the amount of money is decreased, it amounts to virtual robbery of the debtor class."

"It may also be urged that with the progress of improvements in industry, prices tend to fall, and that unless money increases in amount, those who take no active part in these improvements, nevertheless gain the benefit of them."

Prof. Sidney Sherwood, in the " History and Theory of Money," says, p. 225: —

"The ideal that we want, so far as price adjustment is concerned, is to keep prices stable, so that a contract which is payable in one year from now can be paid with just the amount of commodities which will then represent the value stated in the contract of to-day. . . .

"That is what we want, — a stability of prices that persists from one year to another and from one generation to another. . . .

"The object at which we aim is, as it seems to me, a currency which shall keep prices stable, a currency which shall expand, therefore, with the expansion of trade and commerce and development generally, a currency which shall not be lagging behind the commerce and development of the country, and hindering that development, and a currency which shall not, by being too rapidly increased, lead to excessive speculation and to loss."

We may summarize these conclusions in regard to money then as follows: —

Money should have an invariable value.

The test of invariable money value is stability of prices in general.

The value of money depends on the supply of it relative to the demand for it.

The demand for money is variable and uncertain. It is affected by a great variety of circumstances, most of which are beyond control.

The supply is in all cases regulated directly or indirectly by law, and can be controlled.

In any monetary system it is necessary, therefore, that the supply should adjust itself quickly and correctly to any changes in demand, so that prices of all commodities shall, on the average, neither rise nor fall. In this way, and in no other, can an honest money be obtained.

It is believed that these conclusions cannot

be successfully controverted, and, using them as a basis, we now purpose to examine existing monetary systems, and some proposed changes therein, to see in how far they conform to this requirement, and what can be done for their improvement.

CHAPTER III.

EXISTING MONETARY SYSTEMS.

Various substances have been used as money in the past. The "survival of the fittest" has, however, eliminated all but three (omitting fractional coins), and these are used, singly or in combination, at present in all the civilized nations of the world. These three are gold, silver, and paper. Gold and silver are generally used in the form of coins of definite weight and fineness. Paper money is a promissory note issued by the government, or by authorized banks, promising to pay the bearer, on demand, the amount of coin specified on its face.

Where this promise is kept, and coin is paid on demand, the paper is said to be convertible. Where, for any reason, the promise is not kept, and the amount of coin specified will not be given on demand, the paper is called inconvertible or irredeemable.

As the coins which are used, and which are promised to be given in exchange for paper, may be either of gold or silver, or both, the system is said to be a gold standard or a silver standard, according to which one is used, or a bi-metallic standard if both are used under certain conditions. At present, as will be explained in considering that system, there is no country that is really using a bi-metallic standard.

Where the paper money is inconvertible, the coin on which it is based does not circulate with it (for reasons which will appear later), and such a system must be regarded as distinct from the others, no matter whether the basis be gold or silver. Three systems are therefore in use, — the gold standard, the silver standard, and the inconvertible paper. The characteristics of each of these will be considered separately, but, taken as a whole, some facts should first be noted.

Money in all countries is at present essentially a creature of the law. Not only does the government fix the weight and fineness of the coins, but it assumes the right to make the coins, and in some cases to limit the coinage to a certain amount, or to stop coining altogether. It also, in most cases, issues the notes or paper money, and where it does not it controls the issue by laws regulating the banks that do issue them. It controls therefore in all cases the volume of money issued, both by specifying that it shall be made of certain metals which are scarce, and perhaps limiting the coinage of those, and by limiting the amount of paper money that is generally used, to a greater or less extent, in all systems.

There is no international coin or money. Gold and silver when shipped from one country to another go as so much bullion; their value is practically the same whether coined or uncoined. As Walter Bagehot observes, in his work "Lombard Street":—

"Within a country the action of a government can settle the quantity, and therefore the value, of its currency; but outside of its own country no government can do so. Bullion is the cash of international trade; paper currencies are of no use there, and coins pass only as they contain more or less bullion."

Not only is the value of money as a whole, in any country, governed by the law of supply and demand; but each of these three kinds of money, and each of the substances of which they are made, is individually subject to the same great law.

The Gold Standard.

The wide and long-continued use of gold as money has led to a popular impression, current even among well-informed men, that somehow, or in some mysterious way, gold has stability of value and is independent of those fluctuations which they recognize in the values of all other substances. That this is wholly erroneous is admitted by every writer on finance, and quotations are hardly necessary to support the statement that gold varies in value in the same way and is subject to the same law of supply and demand which regulates all other values.

Along with this conception of stability in the value of gold, has grown up a very natural belief that where paper or silver circulated concurrently with gold, so long as they were mutually convertible, gold was the medium which regulated the value of all; and that no matter what the quantities of the others might be, they did not affect the value of the gold or of the money as a whole. This is another popular misconception.

In one sense the gold regulates the value of the money, but only to the extent that it limits, under the existing laws, the volume of the whole by its scarcity. In another and wider sense the value of the gold is itself fixed and controlled by the value of the money in its entirety. The use of gold for money is so enormously greater than its uses for all other purposes, that its value as money fixes its value as a whole, since its money use is by far the largest factor affecting the demand for it.

The demand for money is generally an indiscriminate demand, satisfied with paper money or silver as well as with gold where they circulate together. Hence, every issue of paper or increased coinage of silver in any such country, demand remaining the same, lowers the value of the money as a whole by increasing the supply, and since the value of gold is determined by its value as money, that is lowered with the rest.

The value of gold varies, therefore, with that of the money as a whole of which it forms a part.

In gold standard countries the coinage of gold is unlimited, and — not to speak of the small mint charges — generally free. Under these conditions the value of gold coin and gold bullion are the same, weight for weight.

The silver coin, which is used to some extent in gold standard countries, does not have either free or unlimited coinage at present. Its bullion value is less than its nominal and actual value, which is maintained at a par with that of gold by the limitation of its issue, — just as in the case of paper money, — and by the fact that within the country of issue it does the same work as the gold, just as paper money does. Men will give just as much of any commodity for the silver coin or the paper as they will for the gold, because, their utility being the same, their exchange value must also be the same.

With these facts explained, we can proceed to consider a very important law affecting the value of money and its distribution among different nations.

Gresham's Law.

It was noticed and stated many years ago by Sir Thomas Gresham that full-weight coins would not continue to circulate with clipped, worn, or light-weight ones, and that the latter would drive the former out of the country. This statement has been extended and enlarged into what is known as Gresham's Law, which, as generally formulated, is that a poorer money will drive a better one out of circulation. In this form it is commonly accepted as true, but is often misunderstood and misapplied.

It is, in fact, but a particular case of the more general law that any commodity will seek the market where it is worth the most, where it will exchange for the most of other commodities.

The full-weight coins would exchange for no more in the country of issue than would the light-weight ones (within certain limits), but when it was desired to ship coins to other countries where they were valued by weight and not by tale, the full-weight ones were more valuable, and were, therefore, selected for such shipment, leaving the poorer ones to circulate at home.

The larger application of Gresham's law to money as a whole is as follows:—

The resultants of all the various forces acting on money value through supply and demand evidently must be different in different countries, and thereby may cause the money of one country to rise in value while that of another falls. When this occurs between two countries using the same metal as a part of their money, — that is, either between two gold-standard or two silver-standard countries, Gresham's law immediately operates to bring the two moneys again to a uniform value.

Since the gold varies in value with the money as a whole, it will, under such circumstances, be worth more in the country having the higher money value than in the other, and a flow of gold will set in from the country where it is worth the least to the one where it has the greater value. This flow of gold decreases the amount of money in the country from which it goes, and increases the amount in the other, thus raising the value of money in the one, and lowering it in the other, until they are again on an equality within the limits of the cost of shipping gold from one to the other.

The operation of this law, therefore, tends to make the value of money uniform, and average prices the same in all countries using the same standard.

The gold which thus flows from one country to another does not go, of course, without a return of other commodities in exchange. The operation will be clearer if stated in its converse form.

Since prices and money values are complementary terms, one rising as the other falls, and *vice versa*, a rise in the value of money means lower prices, on the average, in that country. People will buy in the cheapest market, and if prices are lower in one country than in others, they will buy in that country in preference to others; the balance of trade, as it is called, will be in their favour; gold will be sent in payment for the commodities bought; it will increase the money supply and raise prices there, and at the same time it will lower those of the country from which it goes until prices in the two are again on a level.

It must not be supposed, however, as it evidently has been by some, that the operation of this law in regulating prices and making them uniform as between different countries at the same time, has any effect whatever on prices and money values as between two different periods.

An increase or decrease of money value may go on simultaneously in all countries, and no flow of gold be caused; the value of gold would continue to be the same in all countries, yet might be much higher or lower at the end than at the beginning of the period.

To illustrate: the different countries may be compared to several tanks connected at the bottom by pipes, and containing water, the level of which, representing money value, is continually fluctuating with the amounts of water added to or drawn from each of the tanks. If the water rises higher in one tank than in others, a flow will set in from the higher to the lower until all are again on a level; but if the cause of the rise in the one tank continues, or if the cause extends to all the other tanks, the level in all the tanks may be greatly changed.

So the continued preponderance of the forces in one direction, operating either to decrease or increase money value in one country alone or in all together, will raise or lower that value in all the countries which are connected by the use of the common money metal, under a free coinage system. Thus the large discoveries of gold in one country will by this means gradually spread themselves over all gold-using countries. The country where the gold is discovered, is, of course, the richer by the amount discovered, and is none the poorer because of its flow to other countries, for such country receives the same value of other commodities in exchange for the gold.

Through the medium of gold, therefore, general prices are maintained at the same level approximately in all gold-standard countries.

The great defect of the system is, that, because of this mutual bond, no one country can adjust the volume of its money to the demand so as to maintain prices constant. Only by an agreement faithfully carried out by all, or by most of the leading countries, would this be possible. There is no such agreement now existing, nor any likelihood of the leading nations agreeing to do this, and the value of money in all gold-standard countries is the resultant of all the various forces that act upon its supply and demand, with no intelligent attempt to control either; it is, in fact, the foot-ball of politics, selfish interests, and chance.

Neither the annual supply of gold nor the total amount used as money is the principal factor in determining its value. It cannot be doubted that if all the nations now using the gold system were to abandon it, the value of the metal would be but a fraction of its present value, and on the other hand, if all the nations now using silver and paper, in whole or in part, as money, were to change to the gold standard, its value would be increased to many fold what it is now. The legislation, therefore, of all countries is the great factor determining coin value, not alone in the country legislating, but also in all other countries using gold and silver as a basis for their system. The factor next in importance is the extent to which credit is used in the place of money. The total production of gold is so small beyond the amount used in the arts and sciences that it would require a great change in its value, and years of time, for any increased production due to higher value to affect materially the quantity of gold coin in use. The production of gold depends more on chance, and less on its labour

EXISTING MONETARY SYSTEMS. 65

cost, than the production of almost any other commodity; and though it would be, and is, stimulated somewhat by a higher value, there is no such certainty of its increased production being commensurate with the increased labour expended on it as there is in the case of most commodities.

The Silver Standard.

When the money system of a country is based on silver, and that metal has free and unlimited coinage in the mints, as gold has in countries using the gold standard, the same laws apply as in the case of gold. Exactly the same forces operate to affect the volume and value of the money except that the production of silver, its use by other nations, etc., are the factors, instead of gold supply and use. The coin and the bullion are equal in value, weight for weight, and Gresham's law applies the same as it does to gold to regulate the flow of silver from one silver-standard country to another

In some silver-standard countries, however, the coinage is not free and unlimited, the government purchasing the silver at its market rate and coining it in such quantities as it sees fit. In this case the bullion value does not coincide with the coinage value: the latter depends entirely on the amount that is coined, relative to the demand for money, and is independent of the bullion value of the silver. The coin will be of higher value than the bullion, and will not be exported to other countries, as the bullion is equally valuable for that purpose and less costly. It is evident that the value of money is just as dependent on chance, — that is, on a variety of causes too intricate and uncertain to be controlled, — in the case of the silver standard with free coinage as in the case of gold; but as some of the forces acting on silver are different from those acting on gold, one standard may be much more stable than the other.

Bi-metallism.

The theory of bi-metallism — a money founded upon both gold and silver coin — is based upon the fact, before stated, that the value of each of these metals is really determined by the value of the money, as a whole, of which they form a part — their use for money purposes being so much greater than their other uses as to be the determining factor. If all nations, or a sufficient number of the leading ones, agree to coin both gold and silver in any amounts presented, and at the same ratio, the values of each relative to the other will be fixed at that ratio. No other market could be found for either metal at a higher ratio. The plan requires, of necessity, free coinage of both metals by several nations and in the same ratio. If the ratio differs in different countries, or if there are too few countries that are party to the agreement, the operation of Gresham's law will separate the two metals, and cause each to seek the country where it is worth the most as measured in the other. The supply of each metal is independent of the other, and their values, therefore, can only be kept the same by a control and adjustment of the demand thereto.

Where silver and gold are both coined freely at a fixed ratio, if the supply of gold decreases, a portion of the demand for that metal — it being more valuable than silver — would be immediately transferred to silver, raising the latter and lowering the former value, and thus keeping their values at the same ratio. This, however, would not necessarily keep the value of the money constant as regards general commodities, and prices would still fluctuate. The variations would be spread over both metals, and, as shown by Jevons and others, would probably be more frequent, though less extensive.

Theoretically, therefore, a bi-metallic standard is little if at all better than a single standard. Whether it would be better or worse than gold or than silver would depend altogether on the conditions at any particular time, and it is therefore as much the victim of chance as either of the metals alone, so far as providing a money of stable value is concerned.

As already stated, no nation is now using a bi-metallic standard. Countries like France and the United States, which nominally have the double standard, have long since restricted or stopped the coinage of silver and are really on a gold basis, their silver coins being at par with gold and worth much more than their bullion value.

Prior to about the year 1873 these nations, as well as several others, coined silver as well as gold in any amount presented, and all nations using coin were practically on a bi-metallic basis, the ratio between gold and silver values having been maintained at 15½ to 1 (the coinage ratio in Europe) for many years within narrow limits. The United States had adopted the ratio of 15.988 to 1 long before this time, and as a result the silver had all left this country in obedience to Gresham's law, as it was worth more relative to gold in Europe.

About the date above mentioned there was a great change in the coinage laws of several countries. Germany changed to a gold basis, selling a large stock of silver; France and other nations also practically changed to a gold basis by stopping the coinage of silver. As a result of this the relative values of silver and gold changed considerably. The demand for gold increased, and the demand for silver decreased. Silver fell gradually in value relative to gold, and this effect was further affected by large discoveries and greater production of silver.

The United States also stopped the free coinage of silver at about the same time as the other countries, but this had no immediate effect on the relative values of the two metals, for this country was at that time, and for several years afterward, using an inconvertible paper money — no coin of either kind being in circulation. It had, however, a large subsequent effect; for when the United States returned to a specie basis, if the coinage of silver had not been stopped, silver would have been coined in preference to gold, being the cheaper, and this country would have been on a silver rather than on a gold basis.

Paper Money.

Paper money differs radically from coin in one respect. Its circulation is confined to the country of issue. It may indeed be confined to a small part of such country — as in the case of some of the old bank notes — when the solvency of the issuing power is unknown or uncertain. This, however, may be regarded as an abnormal case.

When issued by the Government or by authorized banks whose solvency is unquestioned, it is accepted as freely as coin, and if not so accepted, cannot be considered good money. We shall consider only the case where it is generally accepted.

Being usually a promise to pay coin, on demand, it can, in one sense, be considered honest only when the promise is kept. If the issues are excessive,—that is, if by increasing the volume of the money as a whole its value is lowered so that the coin is worth more in some other country than as a part of that money system,—the coin will leave the country, as has been explained in regard to gold. The paper simply acts as so much gold or silver would act if added to the currency, forcing out a certain amount of coin. Where both metals are used with the paper, the one to go would depend on which was worth the most, relatively, in other countries. If the issues of paper are continued long enough, all the coin will leave the country, and, if still continued, the value of the money will sink below that of the coin, as the paper will not leave the country, but will accumulate, lowering the value with each new issue. The system will then have changed to an inconvertible paper system, the value of the money being no longer dependent on the value of the coin on which it is based, and no longer affected by changes of money value in other countries, but determined wholly by the amount issued, relative to the demands of business in the country of issue.

If the issues continue in excess of demand, the value will lower, even to the point of utter worthlessness; but if properly controlled and limited, the value of the money can be maintained at any point desired far more readily and easily than in the case of a convertible paper and coin system, since many variable forces are excluded when the convertibility is dropped.

The amount of paper money that can be kept at par with coin under a convertible system bears no fixed relation to the amount of the coin. By a proper control of the volume of paper issues their value can be kept equal to coin value, with almost no coin in circulation, or in reserve. An excessive issue of the paper will cause coin to be exported, but this export may be checked, and an import produced by withdrawing some of the paper.

Some control, therefore, may be exercised over the value of money under a convertible system, to make such value constant, but this is evidently limited. If the value of the money is falling, the decline can be checked, and its value made to rise, by withdrawing some of the paper issues; but this will cause an importation of coin, partly offsetting the reduction and checking such rise, and when all the paper has been withdrawn, the power of control by this method ceases. If the money value is rising, an increase of paper issues will stop such rise, but it will cause the exportation of coin; and when all the coin has been exported, the money will cease to be convertible, and the system will have changed to an inconvertible one, — the money still possessing the same qualifications as a measure of value that it possessed in the former case. The only difference is, that in the convertible system the money value is partly determined by the natural causes affecting the supply of coin, partly by the laws and conditions of business in foreign countries, and partly by the legislation at home, restricting the coinage or the issue of paper; while in the inconvertible system it is determined wholly by the control of the issues relative to the demand for money.

This difference may constitute either a merit or a defect, according as the control is intelligent and honest or otherwise.

The disastrous consequences that have resulted at various times from the use of inconvertible paper money, have, in every case, been due to a lack of proper control and to excessive issues, caused generally by the want of a reliable gauge by which to determine the amount that should be issued, and by a misunderstanding of the principles involved.

While paper money, though a promise to pay coin, cannot, in one sense, be called honest, unless the promise is kept; in a larger sense the test of its honesty is its invariability of value.

John Stuart Mill says of inconvertible paper money: —

"In the case supposed, the functions of money are performed by a thing which derives its power of performing them solely from convention; but convention is quite sufficient to confer the power; since nothing more is needful to make a person accept anything as money, and even at any arbitrary value, than the persuasion that it will be taken from them on the same terms by others. The only question is, what determines the value of such a currency; since it cannot be, as in the case of gold and silver (or paper exchangeable for them at pleasure), the cost of production. We have seen, however, that even in the case of metallic currency, the immediate agency in determining its value is its quantity. If the quantity, instead of depending on the ordinary mercantile motives of profit and loss, could be arbitrarily fixed by authority, the value would depend on the fiat of that authority, not on the cost of production.

"The quantity of a paper currency not convertible into the metals at the option of the holder *can* be arbitrarily fixed; especially if the issuer is the sovereign power of the State. The value, therefore, of such a currency is entirely arbitrary."

Prof. F. A. Walker, in his "Money, Trade, and Industry," observes, p. 210: —

"After looking at this subject from every side, I am at a loss to conceive of a single argument which can be advanced to support the assertion of the economists, that paper money cannot perform this function of measuring values, so-called. On the contrary, it appears to me clear beyond a doubt, that just so long and just so far as paper money obtains and retains currency as the popular medium of exchange, so far and so long it does and must act as the value denominator or common denominator in exchange. And I see no reason to believe that in this single respect, hard money, so-called, possesses any advantage over issues of any other form or substance which secure the degree of general acceptance which is necessary to constitute them money."

He says, further, on p. 214 : —

"Such money, so long as its popular acceptance remains undiminished, performs the office of a standard of deferred payments well or ill, according as its amount is regulated."

Paper money is a real economy over gold and silver. Its use substitutes for those coins, that involve much labour in their production, a money of slight labour cost, which, under proper control, performs the functions of money even better than the coin.

If, in any country possessed of the gold basis system, the gold product was wholly deposited in vaults, and paper certificates issued therefor to the amount of the deposits, such certificates, if in proper form and denominations, would answer all the requirements of a circulating medium even better than the gold, and their value would be exactly the same as that of the gold they replaced. By this method, — in a measure, the English system, — the country saves the wear and tear, besides considerable loss of gold, and is better served. The gold thus deposited, except a comparatively small amount shipped abroad at times, would never be called for; its sole purpose would be to regulate by its scarcity the amount of the paper money issued; beyond this purpose, it might as well be iron or lead as gold, or might as well have remained in the mines, from which it was dug at the expense of so much labour, as to be in the vaults.

It would be difficult to conceive of a method of controlling money volume and value more expensive, more clumsy, and more inefficient than this; for, it is to be noted, the control in no way adjusts the volume of money to the demand, so as to maintain a stable value, but merely adjusts the value to that ruling in other countries, — a matter, as we shall see later, of no importance whatever.

CHAPTER IV.

STABILITY OF GOLD AND SILVER VALUES.

Gold-Standard Prices.

Having considered theoretically the limitations and possible merits and defects of the money systems now in use, we shall next consider in how far the money under such systems conforms in practice to the chief requirement, — stability of value.

Economic writers do not claim that either gold or silver is, or has been, of invariable value; but many of them do claim that gold is more nearly invariable than any other commodity, and that it is sufficiently so for money purposes, the changes in value being slight and covering long periods of time, so that from year to year they are almost imperceptible. Other writers claim that silver has been, of recent years at least, more stable in value than gold, and is therefore a better measure of value.

The merits of these claims can be tested, in the same way that the stability of value of any commodity can be tested. by a comparison of the average purchasing power of each metal at different times.

Prof. F. A. Walker, in the work already cited, observes, regarding money value under the gold standard as tested by average prices:—

"Not to speak of the enhancement, many fold, of the value of money through the Silver Famine of the Middle Ages. or of the sudden and extensive decline which has been referred to as taking place between 1570 and 1640, it is estimated by Professor Jevons that the value of gold fell 46 per cent. between 1789 and 1809, that from 1809 to 1849 it rose 145 per cent., while between 1849 and 1874 it fell again at least 20 per cent."

Coming down to more recent times, we have more full and accurate data, and there have been several careful compilations and averages of prices made in different countries. The report of the Finance Committee of the United States Senate, 52d Congress, on "Wholesale Prices, Wages, and Transportation," known as the "Aldrich Report," is doubtless the most accurate and complete examination of prices in this country from 1840 to 1892 that has ever been made. This report also gives for comparison the tables of Soetbeer and Sauerbeck (two of the most distinguished European statisticians), and the table of the *Economist* (London) as to foreign prices, all reduced to the same basis, and to United States money units in gold.

In order to facilitate comparison of these data, the tables have been platted as diagrams in Plate 1. All the tables were prepared by taking the prices of a selected list of commodities for the year 1860 as 100, and calculating the variations in the price of each commodity from the price of that year as a percentage of rise or fall. The average of these percentages for each year represents, therefore, average prices for that year, as compared with 1860, and it is these averages which are platted in the diagrams.

The list of commodities selected by the Senate Committee embraces 223 articles for the years subsequent to 1860. Prior to that time the number was less, varying from 85 to 223, according as data were to be had.

Dr. Soetbeer's table shows prices in the port of Hamburg, Germany, of 100 commodities, mostly raw materials, joined with the export prices of 14 commodities (manufactures) in England, from 1851 to 1891.

Mr. Sauerbeck's table shows English prices of 56 commodities from 1846 to 1891.

The *Economist* table also shows English prices of twenty-two commodities from 1860 to 1892.

The discrepancies between these different authorities, as shown by the variations in the lines of the four diagrams, call for a few words of explanation.

It would naturally be expected that some differences in average prices would exist between different countries, and part of the discrepancies may be accounted for in this way, since there are included in all the tables, among other commodities, such as wood and coal, of which the prices might vary considerably in different countries independently of one another.

Several changes in the tariff in this country during the last fifty years would account for some discrepancies between United States prices and the others. Furthermore, the method by which these tables were in the main prepared, that of taking simple averages of the percentage of rise or fall in price, thus giving to each commodity the same weight in the result, regardless of its importance in commerce, is open to serious objection, and doubtless accounts for many of the discrepancies that exist. For example, the great rise in prices during the period of our civil war, as shown in the *Economist* and the United States tables, above those shown in the other two tables, is doubtless due to the fact that in the *Economist* table, four out of the twenty-two commodities in the list are either raw cotton or cotton manufactures, and the great rise in price of cotton during the war (a rise of from 300 to 400 per cent.) is given an undue importance in the result. The same cause may affect the United States table, to some extent, but a more potent factor in this table is the circumstance that this country, during the period, was using an inconvertible paper money in which all prices were expressed, while gold was a commodity subject to speculation, and the price of which was much affected thereby; and, in reducing currency prices to gold prices, for this table a somewhat abnormal result is produced.

The *Economist* list, it must be said, contains too few commodities to be a reliable index of all.

The United States list is sufficiently large, but the articles selected may be open to some criticism.

The lists of Mr. Sauerbeck and Dr. Soetbeer are preferable, but all are open to the objection, above noted, of not giving a weight to each commodity in proportion to its importance, and none of them can therefore be regarded as anything but approximations to the truth. They embrace, however, the best information on the subject extant.

The United States Committee did, in fact, endeavour to balance their own list in accordance with the relative importance of the articles in another table, but the result is not wholly satisfactory, as the weighting of the averages was done by groups of articles instead of individually for each. It represents, however, probably the most accurate information as to the purchasing power of gold in this country from 1840 to 1892 that can be obtained, and as such has been platted in Plate 2, in a reverse form: that is, assuming that the 223 articles of the list, weighted according to their importance, fairly represent *all* commodities, and that therefore their value as a whole is constant (since the values of all commodities cannot rise or fall simultaneously). The diagram shows the relative values of gold for the different years as a percentage on the value of 1860 taken at 100. In other words, it shows the relative average purchasing power of gold in this country in the different years.

With these explanations of the diagrams, and the limitations of the tables from which they were platted, we can proceed to consider their points of resemblance and what they teach.

It is evident from all of them that a great decline in average prices has been going on, almost continuously, since 1873, in the various commercial countries. This is a fact conceded by all students of prices.

What is equally apparent, however, but does not seem to be so generally appreciated, is the violent fluctuation in prices, or in the value of gold, from one year to another, amounting in many instances to from 5 to 10 per cent. in a single year, and, during the war, to much more. Doubtless if the tables had shown the fluctuation of prices by months or days, instead of the averages for each year, a much greater variation in the value of gold would have been apparent at times, and within a shorter period than a year. Furthermore, the prices of staple commodities (and most of the commodities in all the tables are staples), while representing correctly the *character* of the changes in price of all commodities, would naturally not vary as much as the prices of many more speculative articles of commerce. It is probable, therefore, that gold has varied in value to a greater extent, and within shorter periods, than is shown by the diagrams.

It would be impossible to trace all the various causes that have produced these changes in money value, but a few of the more prominent ones may be indicated as showing their great variety and force.

From 1840 to 1849 a great decline in prices is noticeable, similar to the decline that we know has been going on in the last twenty years. This is doubtless due in both cases mainly to increasing demand for money, caused by growing population and expanding commerce, and which the supply of gold and silver or substitutes therefor did not keep pace with. From 1850 to 1857 prices generally rose, owing to the increased gold production in Australia and California, aided doubtless by the increased use of credit which rising prices always stimulates. The collapse of this credit in the panic of 1857 sent prices down again. The slow recovery from this condition was greatly enhanced by the breaking out of the Civil War, during which thousands of men were destroying instead of producing, thus raising the prices of nearly all commodities by decreasing the supply and increasing the demand relative to gold, while meantime the demand for gold was lessened by the use of paper money in this country. The disbanding of the armies at the close of the war, and the return of labour to productive enterprises, lowered prices rapidly during 1867, 1868, and 1869. From this depression they recovered almost as rapidly in the era of development from 1869 to 1872, the large production of silver from the Nevada and other discoveries during that period assisting greatly in this recovery, and the usual extension of credit at such times also contributing. This credit collapsed in the panic of 1873, and the demonetization of silver by several European nations about the same time prevented any increased production of silver from affecting the decline which then set in, and which has with one or two reactions been continuous ever since.

In the light of the facts, shown by these diagrams, any claim for even approximate stability of value for gold, or for the money as a whole on the gold basis, under the systems now in use, is preposterous. Moreover, the change has been, of late years, of the worst kind. — an increase of money value. If it were steady, its effects could be calculated and discounted to some extent, but caused, as it is, by a variety of forces of varying strengths, the increase is at some times wholly nullified, or even turned to a decrease, by extensions of credit, while again it is doubled in effect by the withdrawal of such credit.

The reason for this great decline in prices, or the increased value of gold, is not far to seek when we consider the relative strengths of the forces acting on gold value. Population, wealth, and diversity of occupations have all increased greatly over the whole civilized world, requiring a much greater amount of money to do the business of the world. There has been, to be sure, as an offset to this, a considerable increase of banking facilities and some greater use of credit paper in its various forms; but all these were in large use prior to 1873, and their increase can hardly have been so great as to meet the demands of growing commerce. Furthermore, of the other forces tending to raise the value of gold, the annual product of that metal has not increased materially, though the demand for it for other than money purposes has increased largely, leaving a less increment to neutralize the waste and to increase the supply of it. And lastly, many countries, as we have seen, about the year 1873 so changed their monetary laws as to use a much greater amount of gold, and a less amount of silver or paper. The United States alone, it is estimated, now uses about $600,000,000 of gold coin, while in 1873 it used practically none.

The effects of this increase in the value of money have been — as the effects of falling prices always are — detrimental and disastrous in all gold-standard countries, to an extent that cannot be measured. Offset at times by increased use of credit, enterprise and industry have been able to rise to a success that an honest money would make their normal condition, only to be dashed down again by the collapse of credit with nothing to take its place.

Silver-Standard Prices.

There is a quite prevalent belief that the value of silver has fallen greatly since 1872. This is a natural sequence to the belief that gold has been stable in value, as the gold price of silver has declined from $1.32 per ounce in 1872, to $0.82 per ounce in 1892 (and since then the decline has been much more). This fall of about 38 per cent. must be deducted from the rise of from 24 to 41 per cent. (according to the different authorities) in the value of gold, in order to show the true change in the value or purchasing power of silver. It is evident, therefore, that the value of silver has been much more nearly constant than that of gold.

This is confirmed by the statement of Mr. David A. Wells, in his work on "Recent

Economic Changes." p. 236. There, Mr. Wells remarks: —

"In exclusively silver-using countries, like India and Mexico, the decline in the value of silver has not appreciably affected its purchasing power in respect to all domestic products and services; but the silver of such countries will not exchange for the same amount of gold as formerly, and it might be supposed that, owing to this change in the relative value of the two metals, the silver of India, Mexico, and other like countries would purchase correspondingly less of the commodities of foreign countries which are produced and sold on a gold basis. But the people of such countries have not thus far been sensible of any losses to themselves thereby accruing, for the reason that the gold prices of such foreign commodities as they are in the habit of buying have declined in a greater ratio since 1873 than has the silver which constitutes their standard of prices."

He also says, in an article in *The Forum*

for October, 1893: "Testimony was given to the recent British Commission on Indian currency, that within the last twenty years half of the silver prices of commodities in India have risen and the other half fallen."

In Plate 2, the dotted line shows the variations in the value of silver since 1872. This diagram is platted from calculations of the percentage of decline in the gold price of silver, taking the price of 1872 as 100 (this was also practically its price from 1840 to 1872, since the ratio of $15\frac{1}{2}$ of silver to 1 of gold was maintained within narrow limits during that time), and deducting these percentages of decline from the percentage of increase in gold value.

In considering the relative constancy in the value of gold and silver, the lines representing each should be compared with the level price line of these metals in 1872. It will be noted that while silver has kept closer to this line than has gold, and on the average has varied but little from it, yet the fluctuations in the value of silver from year to year are quite as marked as in the case of gold.

It will also be noticed that prior to 1872, under a bi-metallic standard, both metals, while maintaining a constant relation to each other, fluctuated in value quite as extensively as either alone has done since.

The facts here shown as to the experience of this and other countries for the past fifty years, bear out the theoretical conclusions before stated, that the value of money, under any of the systems that have been used, is subject to violent fluctuations from year to year, due to a great variety of causes which are entirely beyond control, and that neither silver nor gold singly, nor both combined, has ever proved a reliable standard of value.

CHAPTER V.

CRITICISM OF SOME GOLD-STANDARD ARGUMENTS.

BEFORE proceeding with the main line of this argument, we will digress to notice some of the arguments put forth in support of the stability of the value of gold by those who cannot but recognize the great fall in general prices.

While such writers do not deny the truth of the fundamental principles we have already considered, they either forget or ignore them.

Notable among such writers is Mr. David A. Wells, and as his views may be taken as representative of many others, some statements from his article in *The Forum* for October, 1893, previously mentioned, are here selected for criticism.

In the beginning of that article, as well as in his work, "Recent Economic Changes," he clearly recognizes and states that there has been a great and universal decline in the prices of a variety of commodities within the last thirty years. He claims, however, that such a general fall of prices does not prove that the value of gold has increased, for the reason that, as he endeavours to show, such fall in prices was caused by lowered labour cost of production, due to improved machinery, better methods, greater division of labour, etc. All these facts may be freely admitted; the error lies in supposing that it makes any difference what the cause is. Since value is a relation, it will be altered by a change in either of the terms between which that relation exists, and it is immaterial whether a day's labour produces more commodities in general, and the same amount of gold, or a less amount of gold, and the same amount of commodities in general, as compared with some former period. The value of gold, other things being the same, is greater in both cases. The fact remains that if gold exchanges for more commodities in general than formerly, its value has risen. It is not clear what Mr. Wells' conception of value is, on which his arguments are based. He, however, seems to regard the labour that a commodity will purchase as the measure of its value, since he says, in the magazine article: "And then, in respect to the one thing that is everywhere purchased and sold for money to a greater extent than any other, namely labour, there can be no question that its price *measured in gold* has increased in a marked degree everywhere in the civilized world during the last quarter of a century."

"Measured by the price of labour, therefore, gold has unquestionably depreciated; and can anybody suggest a better measure for testing the issue?"

The fallacy of using labour in any form as a test of value was pointed out in the chapter on value. That the labour a commodity will purchase is not in any way a standard of value, as between two different periods, has been shown by almost every economist from Ricardo down to the present time.

The above quotations, in connection with the following from the same article, bring to light an important phase of the subject, which it may be well to make clear. Mr. Wells remarks: —

"A decline in prices, by reason of an impairment of the ability of the people of any country to purchase and consume, through poverty or pestilence or by reason of the misapplication of labour and capital, *i.e.* waste, . is certainly an evil. But a decline in prices caused by greater economy and effectiveness in manufacture and greater skill and economy in distribution, in place of being a calamity, is a blessing and a benefit to all mankind."

With growing knowledge, and the advancement of the arts and sciences, there is a continual improvement in methods of production and distribution, enabling the same amount of labour to produce and distribute to consumers a far greater amount of commodities in general than it formerly could. This has been conclusively shown in detail by a mass of statistics in Mr. Wells' book. The question arises, to whom should this increased product properly belong?

For the purpose of this inquiry the community may be considered as divided into three separate classes, according to the source from which their principal income is derived; viz. —

(1) Labourers.— including all whose income is principally derived from their work, of hand or brain, whether as wages, salaries, or products directly created.

(2) Employers of labour, — including all whose income is mainly derived from investments of capital directly in productive enterprises in the widest sense of the term. — those who take the risks of business incident to the doing of the work of the community.

(3) *Money lenders.* — those whose income is derived from interest on loans; who, not wishing to take the risks and cares of active business, prefer to loan their capital to others who will do so, accepting as their share of the profits a definite amount as interest.

The incomes of many people are derived, of course, from all three of these sources, but they may be considered as belonging to the class determined by their greatest revenue.

It is evident that labourers should have a share of the increased product that greater skill, improved methods, machinery, etc., create; since labour is the direct cause of such increase, and not only the greater skill but the improved methods are due to labour.

Equally evident is it that the capitalist who has taken the risks of business and whose wealth and enterprise have contributed to the results, should also share in the increased product.

But all considerations of justice and equity forbid that those who, declining to take any risk themselves, prefer to loan their capital to others at a fixed compensation, should receive any share of the increased product which labourers and employers may succeed in creating, beyond such fixed compensation. Justice is satisfied when to them is returned the *value* they loaned with the interest agreed upon for its use.

It must not be forgotten that what is really loaned is capital, — commodities in general, — not money: the money is only a medium for effecting the transfer, and a measure of the capital transferred. What should be returned, therefore, in repayment of a loan is the same amount of commodities in general that was borrowed, — the same value.

It is *not* meant that bond-holders and money-lenders should be entitled to no share in the generally bettered condition of mankind due to lowered labour cost of producing commodities. They should, and in the long run would, receive their full share, through the higher rate of interest that increased general profits would bring if money value were constant, and by this means would obtain a *just* share, determined by open competition and not an unjust share, determined by the insidious device of a varying measure. It *is* meant, however, that the money-lender is entitled to no share in any increased productiveness of labour during the lifetime of his loan, beyond the interest stated. He gets his share of such increased productiveness through the higher interest he will subsequently receive in re-loaning his capital.

If prices of commodities have declined while wages have increased, as Mr. Wells claims, it shows that the labourer, on the whole, has received some share of the increased production, since his wages will buy more of commodities in general than formerly. Whether the employer of labour has also received a share is more difficult to determine; but it is absolutely certain, if prices have fallen, that the money-lender, who is entitled to no share at all, aside from interest, has also received a share, and a very large one in many cases; since the money returned to him in discharge of a debt will purchase a much larger amount of commodities in general than it would when it was loaned; and this share has evidently been drawn from what should have gone to one or both of the other classes, and they are wronged to that extent.

While the labourer may, or may not, have received the share to which he was entitled during the last twenty years, it seems highly probable, from Mr. Wells' statistics and arguments, that it is the employer of labour — who as a rule is the borrower — who has been injured most by the fall of prices.

One of the great aims and endeavours of mankind is to produce the largest amount of commodities possible, with the least labour, — or to lower the labour cost of commodities. It is this lowered labour cost, which is "a blessing and benefit to all mankind," not lowered prices. The two are not the same, nor have they any real connection. Lowered labour cost depends solely on the improvement in skill, methods, machinery, etc., which will go on as well with prices constant on the average, as with falling prices,—in fact, even better,—and the product will then be distributed honestly; while with falling prices the distribution is dishonest.

It is important to keep clearly in mind the distinction between capital and money. That Mr. Wells has not always done so, the following quotation will show:—

"Nobody, furthermore, has ever yet risen to explain the motive which has impelled the sellers of merchandise all over the world, during the last thirty years, to take lower prices for their goods in the face of an unexampled abundance of capital and low rate of interest, except upon the issue of the struggle between supply and demand."

Capital is accumulated wealth devoted to the production of more wealth; money is merely a medium for the exchange and transfer of wealth: they are not synonymous terms. An abundance of capital may exist with a small amount of money (relative to the demand) and consequent low prices, or with a large amount of money and high prices: they have no connection.

The rate of interest, also, has nothing to do with the question. Interest is determined by the amount of capital seeking investment in loans, relative to the demand, and in a time of relative contraction of the volume of money, and consequent falling prices, will, as a rule, be low, since there is less inducement for men to borrow capital to engage in business, and more men wishing to lend. The risks of business are much increased at such a time, and the profits much lessened, and as the rate of interest is determined by the profits of business in general, it will be low also. Mr. Wells, indeed, has recognized this fact elsewhere in his writings, but has evidently forgotten it in the above quotation.

The accumulation of money in banks in times of depression indicates not too much money, but a general belief that its value is rising, or a fear that it will rise; testifying, if to anything, to too little money, in fact. Men do not hold a thing that brings no income unless they expect to profit by its rise.

As to the main point of the above quotation, certainly men accept lower prices for merchandise because of the issue between supply and demand, but the supply of money is as much involved in the calculation as the supply of merchandise. Men accept lower prices — that is less gold — for commodities in general, because gold has increased in value. Mr. Wells further says: —

"No one has ever named a single commodity that has notably declined in price within the last thirty years, and satisfactorily proved, or even attempted to prove, that its decline was due to the appreciation of gold."

No one, of course, could prove by the decline in price of a *single* commodity that money or gold had appreciated; but when a writer admits, as Mr. Wells has done so clearly, that prices in general have fallen, no proof is needed; the statements are but different ways of saying the same thing.

That in order to establish the appreciation of money it is necessary to show that *all* commodities have fallen in price, or that the price experiences of different commodities had harmonized in their decline, as Mr. Wells implies, is manifestly absurd. Even if average prices were constant, there would be continual fluctuations of individual prices, some rising, others falling, and these continue the same with an increasing money value, so that some prices might not alter at all, or might rise even with a rising money value, but others again would decline in a greater degree than if the money value were constant. If the average purchasing power of money is greater, then its value is greater, whatever be the cause.

So much space has been devoted to a criticism of this article because the opinions expressed in it seem to be fundamental and dangerous errors. Moreover, they are given added weight by the reputation and prominence of the author, while they are more or less representative of the arguments of other defenders of the gold standard.

Either Mr. Wells is mistaken in his conception of *value*, and of the standard by which it is measured, or Ricardo, John Stuart Mill, and all other authorities on Political Economy are mistaken in supposing that the value of a commodity is its general purchasing power.

CHAPTER VI.

FOREIGN COMMERCE.

It is claimed by many writers that international trade is carried on upon a gold basis, and that it is necessary, therefore, if a country is to maintain and increase such trade, that it should have its money based upon gold, since its "balance of trade" must be paid in gold.

The idea of foreign trade involved in such statements is a relic of the old "mercantile theory" that the great object of any country was to export as much as possible of its products and receive in return the largest possible amount of gold and silver, — to get gold, in fact, at any hazard. This theory was buried, a century ago, under the weight of Adam Smith's arguments, and every economist since then has helped to bury it deeper; but its ghost still stalks and appears now and again in the form of such statements as the above, and in the common expressions "the balance of trade is against the country," or "the balance of trade is in favour of the country," meaning that gold is being exported or imported, and implying that the one is an injury or the other a benefit to the country.

From a mercantile point of view, there is some justification for these expressions, and for the satisfaction felt at a condition of things requiring the import of gold. As before stated, the value of gold is inversely as general prices in gold-standard countries, and the import of gold means a lowering of its value and a general rise of prices,—which, of course, is what merchants like to have happen; and the export of gold means a fall in prices,—which they dread.

Under a monetary system which maintained prices constant, on the average, the export or import of gold would be of no more importance than the export or import of corn or silk.

From an economic standpoint the term *balance of trade* is a misnomer, and is misleading. Equally misleading and erroneous is the idea that gold or silver is in any way necessary to foreign commerce, or that in consequence of a money being based on one of these metals such trade will be in any way enhanced.

International trade is an exchange of commodities; not, to be sure, a direct barter, but an indirect one. One country exports those commodities which it can produce the cheapest, in exchange for those of other countries that are either not produced at all in the first country, or can be produced only at a greater cost than by import. The immediate force impelling to the export and import of commodities is, in all cases, a difference in their values in the two countries. This is no less true of gold than of other commodities, for gold will never move from one country to another except it be of lower value in the exporting than in the importing country, no matter how much the one may be owing the other. The expressions "balance of trade in favour of," or "against a country," means only that gold is at that time of higher value in one than in another country, by an amount above the cost of shipment, and is being exported or imported because there is a profit in so doing; but this furnishes no criterion whatever of the prosperity of a country. It frequently happens that gold moves for a considerable time from one country to another because of large production of gold in the exporting country. That cannot be considered a bad condition of business or unfortunate for the exporting country, unless the commodities received in exchange are useless, or are wasted. At other times it frequently happens that a country is importing gold, giving in exchange not only other commodities, but promises to pay back the value received, in the shape of bonds and stocks — running in debt, in fact,

This may be a good or a bad thing for the country, as for an individual, according as the value received is profitably used or not. It certainly is no sure indication of real prosperity.

The operations of foreign trade create a great number of claims and obligations on the part of citizens of one country against, as well as in favour of, the citizens of all others. These claims consist of drafts, bills of exchange, letters of credit, etc., and are expressed in every kind of money that exists, whether based on gold or silver, or simply inconvertible paper. Through the medium of foreign exchange banks these claims are offset against each other and cancelled. Between two countries having the same monetary standard there exists what is called the par of exchange; that is, the ratio between the weights of gold or silver in their respective units. The actual rate of exchange — that is, the price which will be paid in one money for claims expressed in another — seldom conforms to this nominal par. The bills of exchange, etc., representing claims of the exporters of one country against the importers of another may be regarded as a sort of commodity, and subject to the law of supply and demand. If one country, A., has more claims against another, B., than B. has against A., then the demand will be stronger for those which are fewer, and the price will rise, and *vice versa*.

The prices of exchange cannot vary from the par of exchange between gold-standard countries much more than the cost of shipment of gold; for if they do, it will become profitable to export or import gold, and this will create new claims balancing the others. The variation of exchange rates within these limits is quite sufficient, however, to cause the *actual* exchange rate, and not the nominal one, to be reckoned on by those engaged in foreign trade.

There exists, and always has existed, an *actual* exchange rate between the money units of all countries, or between the claims expressed therein, no matter what the money was based on; although there cannot be a par of exchange except between moneys based on the same metal. These actual rates are continually varying, even between countries like England and Australia, which not only use the same standard, but a common unit, and there is, therefore, no difference in the practical working of exchange between countries having the same standard and those having different ones.

The inference to be drawn from these facts and theories is, that it would make no difference in the foreign trade of any country if it did not possess an ounce of gold or of silver, or whether its money was based on gold or was inconvertible paper; if the country produces commodities that other countries want, and wants some that other countries produce, the commerce will continue.

If the money of either country is fluctuating in value, relative to the other, to any great extent, it may introduce some uncertainty that will hamper and inconvenience trade,— though to a less extent than a variable money would in its own country, as there are means by which such fluctuations can be guarded against; but unless the changes are sudden and violent, no inconvenience will be experienced, as the actual exchange rates are more or less always fluctuating.

In support of these statements, and as showing that they are borne out by practical experience, the following quotations are given from Mr. Wells' "Recent Economic Changes," in reference to trade between a silver and a gold standard country when the relative values of the two metals were changing quite rapidly. He says, p. 239:—

"Mr. Lord, a director of the Manchester (England) Chamber of Commerce, testified before the Commission on the Depression of Trade, in 1886, that 'So far as India was concerned, it is not necessary to run any risk at all from the uncertainties of exchange.'

Mr. Blythell (representing the Bombay Chamber of Commerce) testified before the same commission, . . . 'There is no difficulty in negotiating any transaction for shipping goods to India and in securing exchange.'"

Mr. Wells says: "Thus from returns officially presented to the British Gold and Silver Commission, 1886, it was established that the trade of Great Britain with India since 1874 had relatively grown faster than with any foreign country 'except the United States and perhaps Holland.'" He also says, of Mexican exchange, p. 241 : "The fluctuations in the price of silver since 1873 — Mexican exchange having varied in New York in recent years from 114 to 140 — would seem, necessarily, to have been a disturbing factor of no little importance in the trade between United States and Mexico; but the official statistics of the trade between the two countries since 1873 (notoriously undervalued) fail to show that any serious interruption has occurred."

During this period, Mexico had a silver standard, while the United States had inconvertible paper for nearly six years of it, and a gold standard for the remaining period.

Mr. Wells further states: —

"In forming any opinion in respect to this problem, it is important to steadily keep in mind the fact that international trade is trade in commodities and not in money; and that the precious metals come in only for the settlement of balances. . . . The trade between England and India is an exchange of service for service. Its character would not be altered if India should adopt the gold standard to-morrow, or if she should, like Russia, adopt an irredeemable paper currency, or, like China, buy and sell by weight instead of tale. . . . Unless all the postulates of political economy are false — unless we are entirely mistaken in supposing that men in their individual capacity, and hence in their aggregate capacity as nations, are seeking the most satisfaction with the least labour, we must assume that India, England, and America produce and sell their goods to one another for the most they can get in other goods, regardless of the kind of money that their neighbours use or that they themselves use."

From the time of the Civil War until 1879, this country, though nominally on a gold and silver basis, was actually using a depreciated paper money. No serious inconvenience was experienced in our foreign trade during the greater part of this time; when the currency was most fluctuating, it doubtless did disturb all business, both foreign and domestic, but this was due to its great and sudden changes, and may be regarded as abnormal, and unlikely under a proper system again to occur.

Walter Bagehot, in his work, "A Universal Money," observes: —

"If France and America had the same currencies as England, it would still happen, as now, that bills on Paris or New York would be at a discount or a premium. The amount of money wishing to go eastward across the Atlantic, and the amount wishing to go westward, would then, as now, settle how much was to be paid in London for bills on New York, and how much was to be paid in New York for bills on London."

It must be evident that if the people of one country have incurred debts to the people of another country expressed in foreign monetary units, nothing but such foreign money will satisfy the claim, and to procure it the debtors must ship some commodity in exchange for it. What this commodity will be, will depend on which is the cheapest — which one the debtor, everything considered, will have to give the least of in exchange for the necessary foreign money, — it may be claims against foreign merchants, or bankers, in the shape of drafts or bills of exchange, or it may be gold, if that is cheaper, or it may be wheat, or cotton, or any other commodity, but it will always be that which the debtor can purchase cheapest. If it be gold, it will be because the debtor can purchase enough gold to exchange for the required amount of foreign money for less of his own money (including transportation and other charges) than he can purchase a sufficient amount of any other commodity, and not because the foreign money is based on gold. In short, the gold differs in no way from any other commodity in such transactions; it is exchanged for the foreign money, which alone can satisfy the debt, precisely as any other commodity.

That both gold and silver may be a convenience at times in international trade is not denied; but they are not a necessity, and their convenience for this purpose is in no way enhanced by their coinage or by their use as a domestic money.

CHAPTER VII.

MONEY IN THE UNITED STATES.

Turning from the consideration of money systems in general to the particular case presented in our own country, we find a most curious system — if, indeed, anything bearing so little evidence of rational adaptation to its purpose is entitled to that name.

The unit of the system is the gold dollar, containing 25.8 grains of standard gold, nine-tenths fine, coined in five, ten, and twenty dollar pieces. There is also a silver dollar, containing 412½ grains of standard silver, nine-tenths fine, the ratio between the two being 15.988 grains of silver to one of gold.

The gold is coined free, in any amount presented. The silver coinage has been restricted for many years, and is now entirely stopped. The silver dollar, however, circulates at par with gold, though its bullion value is only about fifty cents measured in gold, which is the real basis of the system.

In addition to the coin, and circulating on a par with it, are a number and variety of issues of paper money.

(1) United States notes (or greenbacks),— secured only by the credit of the government, except that there is held in the Treasury about 30 per cent. of the amount of these notes in gold as a redemption fund.

(2) National bank-notes, — issued nominally by the various national banks of the country, but practically issued by the government; since they are secured by a deposit of government bonds, are guaranteed by the government, and rest as completely on the credit of the government as the greenbacks do, though in a different way.

(3) Silver certificates. — secured by a deposit of silver bullion.

(4) Gold certificates.—secured by a like deposit of gold.

(5) Treasury notes,— secured by deposits of silver.

(6) Currency certificates.

All of these kinds of paper money, as well as the silver coin, circulate on a par with gold; their utilities being equal, and the demand for money being an indiscriminate one, their values must be equal. As a domestic money, gold cannot have a higher value than the issues of paper money; though it may, however, have a greater value as a commodity for foreign shipment. It is not the fact that these other forms of money may be exchanged directly or indirectly for gold at the United States Treasury that makes their values equal to gold value, but the fact that their *utilities* are equal. They would remain of equal value with gold if the Treasury did not exchange gold for them, so long as any gold remained in circulation as money. A gold reserve, however, is necessary as a precaution in a gold-standard system, but only to the extent of the probable demand for gold for export.

The system as a whole is a ridiculous one, and nearly all its features are wasteful and uneconomic.

Gold coin, as a circulating medium, is not as good as paper; it has a high subjective value, and such use of it is wasteful; it should be kept as a reserve for export purposes. The gold certificates are better, but are also wasteful; since only a sufficient reserve is needed to meet possible demands for export, and this would be far less than dollar for dollar.

The silver coin is open to the same objection as the gold coin as a circulating medium, and the silver certificates to the same objection as the gold certificates, and to the further objection that the silver deposited to secure them is of no use whatever, even as a reserve, for no one would demand silver bullion of the government in exchange for paper money at the present coinage value, when they could purchase nearly twice as much in the open market for the same money. Unless, then, our money should fall in value some 50 per cent., not an ounce of silver will ever be called for at the Treasury in exchange for the paper issues based thereon; and the silver deposits are merely a clumsy and costly method of limiting the volume of the paper money.

The greenbacks, or United States notes, are economical, and if they were variable in volume and under proper control would be a good money.

The national bank-notes are wrong in principle, in allowing private corporations to make a profit from the issuance of paper money. This objection is of no practical importance, at present, as the restrictions and high bond prices have taken away practically all the profit to the banks on the issues, but in so doing have also taken away about the only merit such notes ever had, that of elasticity of volume to some extent. This was a most doubtful merit at best, as the issues were governed by considerations of private profit and not by any desire to make money of stable value. Whatever may have been the merits of the national banking system in the past, the war necessities of the government which gave birth to it, have long since passed away. It can be viewed now only in the light of its present usefulness, and as an issuer of money it is of no use whatever.

Paper money received by deposit of bonds instead of bullion is economical and correct in principle, if controlled in the interests of the public, and not left at the mercy of men whose private interests may be opposed to the public welfare. No such control of the volume of the money is attempted in the case of the national bank-notes, and they are no more secure than are greenbacks, since the ultimate foundation of both is the national credit in one form or another.

Of all our different kinds of money, the only ones susceptible of change in volume to meet the varying demands of commerce are, under existing laws, the gold coin and certificates. These can be changed only by the import or export of gold, or by the product of the mines over and above the amount needed for the arts and sciences, and which must be divided with other gold-standard countries.

The national bank-notes are theoretically elastic in volume, but actually are not so, to any appreciable extent. They require for their issue the purchase and deposit with the United States Treasurer of government bonds, — now at a large premium, — are subject to other charges and restrictions, and are not, as a rule, profitable enough to the banks to cause any increase of the issues above that required by law, except in urgent necessity, and that to a very limited extent.

As a result of these conditions, the country witnessed, during the recent panic of 1893, a resort to every kind of device known to banking and permissible by law, to increase the volume of the currency and meet the enhanced demand for money caused by the utter failure of credit. Certified checks, certificates of deposit, clearing-house certificates, and other devices were resorted to, and even then thousands of solvent institutions over the country were obliged to close their doors, and the industry of the whole country was paralyzed.

The events are of too recent occurrence to need rehearsal here. It is a sad commentary on the wisdom of our legislators that, notwithstanding all the tinkering and patching that our financial system has undergone, and the voluminous debates in and out of Congress for years past, the volume of our money has been so far from keeping pace with the demands of commerce that prices have been falling for a quarter of a century, culminating last year — a repetition, unhappily, of previous experience — in a collapse of the overstrained credit that was vainly trying to do the work of money, and bringing ruin and disaster to thousands.

The condition of our monetary laws to-day is such that, except by the slow increment of gold production, which must be shared by all the world, we possess no means of meeting either the increasing demand for money that expanding population and commerce bring, or the sudden demand that a failure of credit may bring at any time. This, obviously, is a blunder on the part of our law-makers that amounts to a crime.

It is not surprising that under such conditions the industries of the country are crippled and that thousands of men should seek work in vain. Still less surprising is it that in the face of a continually increasing value of money, or decreasing prices of nearly everything else, prudent men choose, as far as possible, to turn their capital into money, lock it up in safe deposit vaults, or let it lie idle in banks, rather than take the great risk that any active use of capital under such circumstances carries with it. When money is increasing in purchasing power from five to seven, and even a higher per cent. per annum, as has been shown to be the case many times in the past, it means that the man who locks his money up in a vault gets that percentage of return for letting it lie idle; or that the man who loans it, even at a low rate of interest,—if a loan with safe security can be found at such a juncture, —makes the five to seven per cent. resulting from the increased value, in addition to what he gets as interest.

Men cannot be blamed for declining to engage in productive enterprises under such conditions, nor for hoarding money instead of using it; the blame lies on the system that not only permits but compels such action.

There is evidently no inducement for men with money to invest it in any productive business with the certainty, under existing conditions, that the record of the past will be that also of the future, and that if a return of confidence again expands credit and stimulates business to a new activity, it is sure to be followed, at no distant day, by another collapse.

It must be conceded, with these considerations in mind, that the imperative need of this country is for a money that shall be at once more honest, more simple, and more elastic, and, at the same time, adaptable to the varying demands of commerce.

Any change in a money system must, of necessity, cause some disturbance of business, and such change should be so devised as to cause the least possible disturbance, and do as little injury to vested interests and existing obligations as possible.

The system chosen should, moreover, be adapted not only to the needs of the present, but also to the possible requirements of the future, so that no change of system will afterwards be called for to meet further changes in demand, and cause again a disturbance of commerce. In short, it should be a system logical, economical, scientific, and permanent, — not a makeshift, to be changed in the next Congress by the addition of another makeshift, in the manner in which our present crazy patchwork of money has been created and maintained.

CHAPTER VIII.

SOME PROPOSED CHANGES IN OUR MONEY SYSTEM.

Of the many plans that have been proposed to correct the evils of our existing money system, it is not necessary to notice here more than two or three. Most of the others are more or less temporary expedients which, even if meritorious, fall so far short of an adequate or permanent solution of the problem as to merit little attention.

The change which has been most urgently advocated is a return to the free coinage of silver.

It is not proposed to enter into any extended discussion of the merits or demerits of this proposition. Much has been written on the subject already, most of it, unfortunately, from a partisan standpoint, and ignoring all facts and principles, however well established, which did not agree with the views advocated. This, it may be said, is equally true of both sides to the controversy. It seems desirable, therefore, to point out how the principles we have already investigated apply to the question.

Those who advocate free coinage of silver claim that the value of gold has increased since free silver coinage was stopped, while the value of silver has remained more nearly constant. This claim, as we have seen, is correct. They claim not to desire to substitute silver for gold in the coinage, but to use both together at the ratio of 15.988 to 1, under a bi-metallic system, increasing the volume of money, and thereby raising prices to a higher level.

Their opponents say that free silver coinage will drive gold out of the country and the value of our standard will at once fall to the present bullion value of silver (about 50 to 60 cents, measured in gold), and that bi-metallism is only practicable by agreement between the leading nations.

That free coinage of silver would result in driving gold from the country has been largely denied by the advocates of that measure. In this denial they make a great mistake, not only because the statement is strictly true, as theory and experience in the past have alike shown, but also because it would accomplish what they are aiming at, and is the only way in which it can be accomplished through silver coinage. The increase in the volume of money here would raise prices, and the flow of gold to other countries would raise their prices also, and thus a general rise of prices and a lowering of the value of gold, would result.

The gold-standard advocates have also made an error in supposing that free silver coinage would result in the *immediate* fall of our standard to the present bullion value of the silver dollar.

It would be rather difficult to trace the immediate effects of such a measure, as several conflicting forces would be brought into play, the relative strengths of which could not be foretold. It seems probable, however, that the first effect would be a large rise in the price of silver bullion, and a hoarding of gold, followed by its export in exchange for silver. For a time this would cause a fall in prices of other commodities, followed by a rise, as the new coinage began to fill the place of the gold hoarded and exported. However this might be, it can hardly be doubted that the final result would be a rise in prices of commodities — including silver — as measured in gold, or a fall in the value of gold all over the world as measured by commodities. Our money would probably remain at a slight depreciation below our gold standard, while both together would gradually lower. This condition would be made manifest by gradually increasing prices, and would continue either until all the available gold had been exported, or until the rising value of silver met the falling value of gold at the coinage ratio of 15.98 to 1. Whichever of these results took place would depend on the relative amounts of gold available for export and of silver for import, and could hardly be foretold. It seems more than likely, however, that the gold would all be exported. In this case, the country would have the silver standard, and the value of the dollar would be somewhat lower than the value of a gold dollar then, and considerably lower than the value of a gold dollar now, but also considerably higher than the bullion value of the silver dollar is now.

If the two dollars reached a parity at their coinage ratio before all the gold was exported, the country would have not only a bi-metallic standard, but would practically force such a standard on the rest of the world, as long at least as the gold supply held out. If foreign nations returned also to the free coinage of silver, they would either have to change their ratio to agree with ours, or, if they kept their present ratio of 15½ to 1. the silver would gradually leave us in exchange for their gold.

The fear of a sudden fall in the value of the dollar, as a result of free silver coinage, is not justified. The value of the dollar would fall gradually as the volume of the money increased,— as would be made manifest by gradually rising prices,— except that this fall would be more or less counteracted at the start by a hoarding of gold, which would decrease the supply of money, and perhaps by a disturbance of credit, which would increase the demand for it. The first effects might be, therefore, an increase instead of a decrease of money value.

It would probably not make so very much difference whether bi-metallism or the single silver standard was the final result. The value of the dollar would not be greatly different in the two cases. Before we reached a silver basis we would have exported some five or six hundred millions of gold, and bought its equivalent in silver, securities, and commodities, and the result would necessarily be a great advance in the value of silver, and a corresponding fall in the value of gold,—the reverse, in fact, of what happened when Germany and other nations changed from a silver to a gold basis. Whether, therefore, this country were able or not to restore the parity of the two metals at the present coinage ratio, the departure from such parity would not be nearly so great as it now is. Provided that the volume of the uncovered paper money remained the same as now, and that, when the change was finally accomplished, credit were used to the same extent as before, the value of the dollar would be somewhere between the present bullion values of the gold and silver dollars, and probably nearly as high if the result were the single silver standard as it would be if bi-metallism were accomplished.

The merits and demerits of the plan may be summed up as follows: —

The change would necessarily cause a great disturbance of business, which might result, at first, in a lowering of prices, but would eventually result in a gradual but considerable increase of general prices, and a stimulation of industry.

Debtors would be benefited considerably, and creditors wronged considerably, especially in short-time obligations; though the long-time ones — those that had run for a number of years — would not be affected so much.

Once established, the money value would probably be less variable than gold has been, and rather more variable than silver has been in the past, but this could not be said with certainty, as the money value would continue to be the result of a variety of forces, of which no one could predict or control the strength.

The inconvenience of so bulky a metal in large amounts would almost necessitate its deposit in vaults and the issue of paper money

PROPOSED CHANGES IN MONEY SYSTEM. 145

in its place for actual circulation. If this paper were issued only to the amount of the silver deposited, it would be a most uneconomical system, since the greater part of the silver might evidently just as well be in the ground from which it was dug, so far as any real use was concerned. If paper were issued in excess of the silver deposited, it would not make a market for very much more silver than we now use, and the value of silver would be raised but little.

The value of the money would therefore depend largely on the use that was made of paper in connection with it. Without some control of the volume of the money besides the control the supply of silver would give, its value would continue to fluctuate at all times, and greatly so in times of panic, as it always has done. With proper control the silver is wholly unnecessary, as its only use is to limit the volume of the money, and this can be done far more cheaply and efficiently in other ways.

Little need be said of the "Greenback" or fiat money proposals, so prominent some years ago, though they are seldom advocated now. Their only merit was a dim perception of the fact that gold and silver are not necessary to a money system. Their errors were that they failed to provide any standard by which money value could be tested, or any control had of its volume. They also failed to recognize the fact that money value is wholly dependent on money volume.

Various plans have been proposed for changing our money system by increasing the issues of bank-notes. One of these plans is to repeal the present prohibitory tax on State bank-notes, which would, of course, result in the issue of such notes to any extent that was profitable.

Several other plans propose to increase the issue of national bank-notes by removing some of the present restrictions, and allowing the banks to pledge other securities than United States bonds as a guarantee of their circulation, or by allowing their capital to serve, in part, as such guarantee.

All of these plans are merely makeshifts, and merit little attention. Considered, however, only as makeshifts, and with reference solely to the claims they advance, they are of no permanent benefit to the public. They only allow the banks to make a profit that should go to the community. It is claimed that the money volume will be made more elastic by these issues. This claim does not appear to be justified by an analysis of most of them, and, so far as it holds good in any of them, it is a most dangerous feature. If the issues are made profitable to the banks,— and otherwise there would, of course, be no issues, as they are not compulsory,— then the banks would undoubtedly increase them to the full limit allowed by law at any time. If they were limited so as to be profitable only when interest rates were high, then, when times were prosperous, prices rising, and profits large, the interest rate would be high, and the increased issues would enhance the "boom." When, however, the inevitable reaction came, and prices began to fall, and credit to be withdrawn,—the time, most of all, when more money would be needed,—the banks would not only be helpless to increase their issues, but would very likely reduce them, because of the increased risk at such times, and the fact that, in times of depression and declining prices, interest rates are apt to be low also.

Elasticity of volume is a most necessary feature of a money system, when it is rigidly controlled, to make money value constant; but it would be a most dangerous feature when the control was governed by the desire only to make the most profit. It would simply result in a greater fluctuation of money value than there is now.

We have, so far, examined these various plans for amending our faulty money system rather in regard to the truth of their pretences than in regard to the requirements of an honest money. In this latter respect, all the plans ignore the necessity for an invariable standard of value, and provide no method for controlling the volume of money, and adjusting it to the demand, as might be done, to some extent, even with the gold standard. The general decline of prices could not be prevented, though some of the fluctuations might.

The fact must be faced, that any attempt to increase the volume of money in this country, and thereby raise our prices above those of other countries, or to maintain our prices in gold constant, while those of other countries are declining, can result only in the export of gold. This might not happen at once, for it takes time for Gresham's law to operate, but it would be inevitable. It would probably be delayed somewhat by foreign speculation in our securities, — always a powerful factor in determining the value of our money, — but it would come; and the resulting depression would be all the greater for the delay and the height of the prosperity that preceded it.

So long as our money is based on a metal that forms a part of the money of other countries, under a free coinage system, so long will the value of our money fluctuate under the influence of foreign monetary legislation, wars, panics, and a hundred forces beyond our control.

Only by divorcing our money from that of other countries can we control it, and only by controlling it can it be made honest money.

CHAPTER IX.

A NEW MONETARY SYSTEM.

In the development of commerce from simple barter between savages up to its present complicated form and enormous volume, an evolution is apparent, similar in character to that which has taken place in the organic world. In both the change has been from the simple and homogeneous to the complex and heterogeneous. In both it has been a differentiation of the functions of the several parts, accompanied by an increased sensitiveness of the whole.

The primitive form of commerce, direct barter, may be compared to one of the lowest forms of animal life, in which all parts are alike mouth and stomach, and which if cut into pieces, will exist, severally, as a complete animal; while modern commerce, with its various parts, each with a separate function, and its highly sensitive organism, is more like a human being, in which each part is adapted to the work it has to perform and is dependent on all the others, so that the failure of any one to do its work cripples all the rest.

Just as the cutting or maiming of a low form of animal life is of little damage to it, while a far less injury, relatively, would kill or seriously maim a man, so an injury to commerce, that in a primitive form would amount to little, in our modern highly developed system would cripple it greatly. Money is one of the most important parts of our industrial system, — the very life-blood, in fact, — and if, for any reason, it fails to perform its functions fully and completely, the consequences are far more disastrous than they would have been under the more primitive systems of the past.

Along with the evolution of commerce in general has gone an evolution of money and the mechanism of exchange. As the volume of traffic grew larger, the use of the bulkier commodities as money was gradually abandoned for the more valuable metals. In time, even these became too bulky and inconvenient for use as a medium of exchange, and credit, in its various forms, now does the work of money, as to this function, to a far greater extent than money itself does, and even the money itself is mostly a paper money,—a sort of certified credit.

As previously stated, about 95 per cent of the bank deposits are in forms of credit, and of the actual money deposits only about one-tenth is gold, the balance being paper money and silver; so that, on the strength of these estimates, only .6 per cent of the exchanges of commodities are effected through the direct use of gold.

This evolution of money, however, has been almost wholly confined to the one function, a medium of exchange; there has been no advance for centuries in regard to the other function, a measure of value. Men have continued to cling to the fiction that gold was a standard of value, and that, so long as their monetary system was based on that metal, their unit was of invariable value. We have seen how little ground there is for this claim; that a gold basis for our money is not necessary to our foreign commerce; and how small a part gold really plays in domestic commerce as a medium of exchange. Is it not about time, then, to abandon the fiction that gold is either a standard of value or a medium of exchange, in any proper sense of the terms, and to take a forward step in the evolution of money by adopting a more scientific standard of value, and making the money, as a measure of value, conform thereto?

Professor Jevons, in "Money and the Mechanism of Exchange," in the chapter on "A Tabular Standard of Value," inquires whether it is not possible to have a standard based on a large number of commodities,—a "multiple legal tender," as he terms it,—and concludes that the plan would resolve itself into those severally proposed by Joseph Lowe in 1822, and, independently, by G. Poulett Scrope in 1833, and by G. R. Porter in 1838. These plans were practically alike. Recognizing the fluctuations of money value, and the injury done especially to long-time debts thereby, they proposed that tables be prepared showing the variations from year to year of the prices of the principal commodities, taking into account, also, the amounts sold. These tables were to be used for reference, to ascertain in what degree a money contract must be varied so as to make the purchasing power of the money returned equal to that loaned. The plans seem to have been only suggestions, and the details not worked out. Professor Jevons speaks favourably of them, as perfectly sound in principle, and the difficulties in the way as not considerable. He suggests a method by which the average prices of the commodities could be computed, and closes with the statement: "Such a standard would add a wholly new degree of stability to social relations, securing the fixed incomes of individuals and public institutions from the depreciation which they have often suffered. Speculation, too, based upon the frequent oscillations of prices which take place in the present state of commerce, would be to a certain extent discouraged. The calculations of merchants would be less frequently frustrated by causes beyond their own control, and many bankruptcies would be prevented. Periodical collapses of credit would no doubt recur from time to time, but the intensity of the crisis would be mitigated, because, as prices fell, the liabilities of debtors would decrease approximately in the same ratio."

Prof. F. A. Walker, referring to these schemes, and to similar ones proposed by Count Soden and by Professor Roscher in Germany, criticises them as too cumbersome for general use. but thinks they might be advantageously employed for long-time contracts. The criticism is evidently just; not only are the plans too cumbersome, but they only partially accomplish what is needed. They contain, however, the germ of a plan which it is believed would be both more effective and less open to the criticism mentioned. Long and short time contracts, and cash transactions, are too intimately connected to make it possible in practice to use different and varying standards for each.

Since the values of all commodities constitute the only true standard of value, as close an approximation to this standard as possible should be adopted as our standard of value.

Since the value of the circulating medium — the money — depends on supply and demand, the supply should be so controlled that the value of the money would always correspond with that of the standard adopted, and since paper money is the cheapest, the most convenient, and the only money entirely free from outside influences affecting its volume and value, our currency should be a paper money.

The following is given as the outline of a plan embodying these features and requirements.

The Standard of Value.

Let a commission be appointed by Congress to select a sufficient number of commodities, say, one hundred, to be used as a standard of value.

This selection should comprise the commodities most largely bought and sold and most independent of each other in their values; preference should be given to those which are products of this country, — but foreign products should also be included, — and to those which are reliable in quality and of which the prices are regularly quoted — such, for instance, as wheat, corn, oats, rye, barley, cotton, wool, tobacco, rice, gold, silver, lead, copper, tin, iron, steel, cotton and woollen cloths, leather, hides, lumber of various kinds, sugar, beef, pork, mutton, etc.

The aim should be, while not including all commodities, which would of course be impossible, to include a sufficient number and of such varied kinds as to fairly represent all. Less than a hundred might be sufficient, or it might be better to take more than that number.

With the aid of statisticians, the average price of each of the commodities selected, in their principal markets for a few years past, should be ascertained and tabulated. The commodities, of course, should be of specified grade and quality, and in a specified market, but not necessarily the same market for all.

The length of time over which the average of prices should extend would be determined as closely as possible by the average length of time that existing indebtedness had run. (The reason for this will be explained later.) In addition to the average prices of each commodity, the approximate amount or value annually consumed in this country, should be ascertained.

From these data, a table should be prepared showing the amount one dollar would have purchased, on the average, of each of the commodities for the time determined, and from this a final table should be made taking such multiples of the amounts found in the previous table as should represent their proportionate consumption, — in other words, their relative importance in trade.

For example. suppose the time selected were five years, as representing twice the average time existing debts had run; that during that time one dollar would have bought, on the average. 1.25 bushels of wheat, or 3 bushels of corn, or 100 pounds of pig iron, or 10 pounds of cotton, all of specified grade in specified markets; that, further, the importance of each of these commodities in the trade of this country was in the approximate proportions of 5, 3, 2, and 1, respectively.

Then the final table would show: —

5 ×	1.25 =	6.25	bushels of wheat =	$5.00
3 ×	3 =	9	bushels of corn =	3.00
2 × 100	= 200		lbs. of pig iron =	2.00
1 × 10	= 10		lbs. of cotton =	1.00

Total, $11.00

Considering these four commodities only, the dollar, as the unit and standard of value of our system, would be defined by law as one-eleventh of the sum of the values of 6.25 bushels of wheat, 9 bushels of corn, 200 pounds of pig iron, and 10 pounds of cotton. This illustrates the method of arriving at, and the definition of, the standard. Extended to all the commodities selected, the definition would be the same with the substitution of the proper figures.

This would evidently provide a standard that would closely represent the average purchasing power of one dollar for the time selected. As to the length of time over which this average should extend, if there were no such thing as existing debts, it would clearly be of little importance what the value of the unit selected was, just as it would be of no importance now whether the foot or the pound had been originally fixed at greater or less than their present length and weight; but because of the vast amount of existing indebtedness, the value of the unit that is to be made permanent should be most carefully fixed at the value it had when such indebtedness was created, so as to do as little violence as possible to outstanding obligations. The fact that in the past the debtors have been wronged to the advantage of creditors, by an increasing value of money, furnishes no excuse for a reversal of this injustice and a wronging of creditors by permanently fixing the value of the dollar at what it was twenty or thirty years ago. The debtors and creditors of to-day are not the same individuals who stood in those relations at any time in the past, and two wrongs do not make a right.

The object should be, therefore, to determine as closely as possible how many years, on the average, existing debts have run, and take twice that period for the total length of time over which our prices should be determined. The average of the prices would then correspond with what it was when average debts were incurred.

This would doubtless work a slight injustice to those whose debts were of longer standing,—though a less injustice than they are subject to now,—and would be a slight injustice to the creditors of more recent date; but as some time would be occupied in getting the system to work, so that the actual value of the money would correspond with the standard, the injustice would be more or less distributed, and would at most be slight. It would be substituting only a gradual rise in prices for the decline that has been going on, until prices were back to the level of perhaps two or three years before, and then fixing the level at that point.

The Medium of Exchange.

After the statistical work outlined above had been completed, Congress should repeal the present monetary laws, substituting for the definition of the "dollar" the new definition agreed upon. It should then provide a currency or money to take the place of that now used. This currency should be a paper money similar to our "greenbacks." It should be a legal tender for all debts public and private (except, of course, such as by their terms are payable in gold). In fact, the only difference between such notes and existing "promises to pay" of the government would be that the new notes, as is evident from the new definition of the dollar, would be promises to pay *a definite value,* and not a definite quantity of one commodity of uncertain value.

The notes could be made redeemable *in any commodity at its current market price,* and should contain a pledge, on the faith of the government, that the amount of the currency in circulation would be at all times so controlled by the government that its actual purchasing power would conform to the standard on which it was based.

To carry out this pledge, it would be necessary to have a small corps of statisticians who would receive and tabulate the current market prices for each day; and who would calculate therefrom the aggregate prices of the specified quantities of all the commodities constituting the standard,— in similar form to the final table before mentioned, and of which an example has been given. If this aggregate for any day were more or less than the total of the standard table, it would show that prices in general had risen or fallen, and some money should be withdrawn from circulation, or more issued until the daily total corresponded with the standard total.

Doubtless several plans might be proposed for putting such a money into circulation and controlling its volume. The following seems to commend itself by its simplicity and effectiveness of control, for at least a part, if not all, of the issues, viz.: The money to be loaned by the government on approved securities, such as their own bonds; other bonds of states, counties, cities, railroads, etc.; warehouse receipts, gold and silver deposits, etc. First-class commercial paper, when guaranteed by solvent banks, might also be taken, especially in case of threatened panic. In short, such securities as would be considered the safest for banks and trust companies to loan upon, all under such proper restrictions and safeguards as would insure their safety as collateral. The rate of interest charged for such loans to be a *variable one*, decreasing as prices tended to fall, and increasing as they tended to rise, and without other restriction. This would absolutely control the volume of money, within narrow limits, since more would be borrowed at a lower, and less at a higher rate, of interest, yet the control would be elastic.

While the loans should be for short time, they could be renewed at pleasure, and as often as desired, at the current rate of interest, the security remaining good.

Such a plan would not interfere with general banking business to any considerable extent. In order to prevent monopoly, the loans should be open to all on equal terms, and the list of approved securities acceptable as collateral should be made as wide as possible, consistent with safety. It would probably be found by experience, however, that the principal borrowers direct from the government would be the banks, who would re-loan the money (at a sufficiently higher rate to pay them for their trouble) to their customers, on local securities, commercial paper, etc., as they now do.

In fact, the present system of national banks could be made, with few changes in the regulations governing them, a most valuable adjunct to the plan as a distributing agency, and the plan is one that it would seem ought to meet with approval. They would, it is true, lose their present note circulation, but that, under existing laws and conditions, is of little or no profit to them. They would gain by its being unnecessary for them to keep so large a reserve of cash on hand as they are often obliged to do now; for not only would the whole financial system be more stable than now, but they might safely be allowed to carry a part of the present 15 to 25 per cent. reserve, required by law, in such securities as they could at all times use as collateral with the government. They would gain even more by the security such a system presents against panics and senseless runs, which so often compel solvent banks to close their doors. In short, the government would act toward the banks, not as a competitor, but rather in the relation that the New York clearing-house has several times acted toward its members in times of panic, by the issue of clearing-house certificates, — a quasi-money that helped them in time of need. The government would not be subject to the limitations of the clearing-house, however. The money it loaned would be, unlike clearing-house certificates, a legal tender everywhere; and the protection would extend to all the banks of the country. The government would act toward the banks in somewhat the same way as they act toward individuals, or as the Bank of England acts towards the other English banks, as a sort of reserve agent. In this case, however, the resources as to money would be unlimited. In the manner of regulating the volume of money, also, this plan would resemble that of the Bank of England, since that institution attempts in a feeble way, and prompted doubtless by self-interest, to regulate the volume of money, to some extent, by raising the discount rate when the volume is decreasing, as evidenced by exports of gold, and lowering the rate when gold is being imported.

If it were impossible or inexpedient to loan in the above manner all the money the country required, a sufficient amount could be so loaned as to give an absolute control of the volume, and to regulate its value at all times, and the balance could be issued in exchange for the present greenbacks, and for interest-bearing bonds of the government, thus converting a part of the interest-bearing debt into a permanent non-interest-bearing one.

It is evident that the control of such a system should rest with the government, and not be left to any banking institution; for a bank would be more influenced by considerations of profit than of proper control in the interests of all. The interest received by the government would be a minor consideration, the control of the volume being the main object, and the rate of interest a means merely to that end. The people, besides, would have at all times a greater confidence in notes issued directly by the government than they could have in notes issued by any bank, however strong.

The department of the government to be charged with this issuing function should, of course, be entirely distinct and separate from the other departments. Its sole business should be the maintenance of an honest money. It should have no connection with the general expenditures of the government, further than to pay into the Treasury such profits, in the way of interest, as might be received. The government expenses should be met, as they now are, by the receipts from taxes and duties, or, if these were insufficient at any time, by borrowing money on its bonds. Under no circumstances should money from the issuing department ever be taken for the expenses of government, except in the same way that banks or individuals might receive it, and never then to an extent that would raise average prices.

The legal tender provision of the notes would be necessary only as specifying the medium in which payment of debts should be made, to prevent misunderstanding, and for the protection of debtor and creditor alike. The new dollar being a quantity of value, and not of a specified commodity, a loan might be returned in any commodity of that value but for some such provision.

The provision could in no case wrong a creditor, for what he would receive in payment of the debt would be a positive guarantee to deliver him the *value* specified in any commodity he chose. Making the money redeemable in any of the commodities on which it is based would be only a form, and might be omitted; it is suggested merely as obviating any objections to an irredeemable money. Of course the government would never be called upon to so redeem money, since the holder of it could exchange it for the commodity wanted in the open market to equal advantage. No reserve of commodities of any kind need be kept, therefore, for redemption purposes. One great difference between this plan and existing systems will, of course, be seen at once: the present system promises a definite amount of gold, and must, therefore, keep a gold reserve; but as no one really wants the gold, except to exchange for commodities, this plan proposes to do away with the necessity for a gold reserve by guaranteeing that the money can be directly exchanged for such commodities at the current market price, — which is all that can be done with the gold, — and that the average purchasing power of such money shall not vary as gold does.

It must not be supposed that this plan contemplates any control of individual prices. Such will be free to fluctuate in accordance with the law of supply and demand, as they now and ever must do, regardless of the monetary system used. It would not be desirable, even if it were possible, to make individual prices constant; but what is desirable and possible, and what it is believed this system would accomplish, is to relieve the prices of all commodities from the fluctuations due to changes in value of the one commodity by which all others are measured; to make the money — the one commodity which no one wants except for measuring the value of and exchanging for other commodities — of constant value. The prices and values of gold and silver would then depend on their use for other than money purposes, or for money purposes in other countries, and if the value of either metal should fall, or fail to continue to rise, there would be no room for complaint that it was being discriminated against by the laws, since all commodities would be treated alike, and the demand for none increased over what it would otherwise be by its selection for monetary uses.

It is evident that gold could still be used as a hoard of value, if desired, but such use would in no way interfere with the volume of money, as it now does. Neither would the hoarding of money itself affect prices and cause business stagnation as is the case now. The reasons for such hoarding would be mostly done away with, but if any should remain and the money be hoarded, the government would at once issue as much more as was needed to supply the deficiency so created, thus maintaining its value constant, and when the money hoarded was again put in circulation the government would withdraw a portion of it if it were excessive in amount.

The exchange of the new money for the existing kinds would be a matter of practical financiering, presenting no unusual difficulties. This need not be enlarged upon.

The gold certificates should be redeemed with the gold now held for that purpose. This gold, as well as that now in private hands, would thereafter take care of itself.

The silver dollars, and all forms of paper money, should be redeemed in the new money, dollar for dollar; the paper money should be cancelled, and the bullion — both gold and silver — sold gradually, with due regard to the effect of such sales on the prices of gold and silver, especially the latter. The proceeds of such sales in the new money should also be retired from circulation.

As a final result, the new money issued would

all be in the form of loans to banks or individuals, except to the amount used in redeeming the uncovered paper now outstanding, less the reserve fund (and some loss that would result from the sale of silver below the price paid for it). This net balance of the new money issued, above what was issued as a loan, could be left as an uncovered paper issue, as it now is; but for the sake of uniformity it would be better to make all the money a loan issue, in which case it would be necessary to issue bonds to take up such amount. It represents now, of course, a remnant of our war debt, not refunded. No increase of interest charges would result from funding it in bonds, for the interest on the bonds would be offset by the interest on the equal amount of extra money that would be loaned in that case. It would make no difference as regards this general plan which of the two methods were adopted.

This plan should not be confounded with any "fiat money" or unlimited "greenback" proposals. Its main point is directly the opposite of these, to secure a more complete control of money volume. It is not an attempt to make something out of nothing, or to create value by government fiat or authority where none existed before, or to coin the government's credit,—although there is no valid objection to doing the latter when properly limited.

It is simply an exchange of credit, analogous to the operation of every bank. The government would loan a command over immediate goods (represented by its promise to deliver such goods on demand) in exchange for a promise to return such command over goods at a future time, and secured by a deposit of collateral; and in payment for the difference between the value of present and future goods it would charge interest. This is precisely what the loan department of every bank does. Every man who accepted the money in payment for goods would deposit, for the time being, with the government the command over commodities in general which he owns; the money being his certificate of deposit. This would constitute the fund from which the loans were made, just as the deposits in a bank constitute, in the main, its loan fund. When the money was used to purchase goods, it would be redeemed, so far as the purchaser was concerned, and the claim would be transferred to the seller of the goods, who in turn would become a depositor.

Like every bank, the government would rely on the probability that all claims against it would not be presented for payment at once, but this probability would amount to a certainty in the case of the government, for there would be no probability of *any* of the claims being presented for direct redemption, as every one who had goods to sell would redeem the notes, so far as the holder was concerned.

The honesty of the government as an agent for all the people is, of course, assumed in this plan; but the credit of the government, in any other than a trust capacity, is neither assumed nor involved, since it would hold secured claims against others for every dollar issued (unless, of course, a portion of the money was left as an unsecured issue, which, as above stated, is no necessary part of the plan).

Money, in its ultimate analysis, is simply a claim which the holder has against society for goods in general. It is the faith that such claim will be recognized, and its value be stable, that gives currency to all money.

This faith, in the case of coin, is based wholly on long custom and usage; in the case of paper money, it rests on such custom joined to the pledge — express or implied — of the issuer of the paper.

Selling is simply the exchange of a particular thing for a command over things in general, and the reverse — buying — is the exchange of the general command over goods for some particular good.

In all existing moneys, this claim is one only of usage, and its value is variable. In the plan proposed it becomes a definite promise of such goods in general, and to a definite value, the government being the guarantor.

The plan closely resembles the present national banking system, but broadened and improved, and with the objectionable features of that system removed.

CHAPTER X.

MERITS AND OBJECTIONS CONSIDERED.

The foregoing chapter is only an outline, but is believed to be a sufficiently definite one to show the feasibility of the plan.

Merits of Plan.

The merits of the plan are believed to be:—

(1) It furnishes a standard of value as nearly invariable as it is possible to obtain in practice.

(2) It gives a medium of exchange conforming in value closely to the standard, one which is cheap, convenient, elastic, and to be had in any amount needed.

(3) It would prevent panics. This may seem

an extravagant assertion, but further consideration will show that it is well founded. A panic, whatever the cause, manifests itself as an unreasoning fear and distrust, which prevents credit from doing its usual work, and creates an excessive demand for money; not only because the money is then needed by each individual who demands it, but because each is afraid if he does not get it then he will not be able to get it when he does need it. It means a hoarding of money, a great rise in its value, or, as generally expressed, a great fall in prices. All this is enhanced by the knowledge of the limited amount of money; in fact, the fear is not so much of the ultimate solvency of banks and business institutions as of the fact that there may not be money enough to go round, and that those who are not first will be at a disadvantage. The plan proposed will, in the first place, prevent the growth of any such fear up to the panic point, by the knowledge that the government stands ready to furnish any amount of money that may be needed to maintain prices; and, in the second place, if by any chance such a fear should arise, its first manifestation would be falling prices, which would at once bring an increase of money volume to meet the demand. It is well known that nothing will so effectively prevent a panic that is impending, or check one that has already begun, as the assurance that the institutions involved stand ready to meet any demands that may be made upon them. A run could hardly originate on a bank, believed to be solvent, were it known that it could obtain at any moment all the money needed for the emergency. An element of certainty and stability would, by this protection, be given to all banks, and through them to all solvent and legitimate business institutions, which is now sadly lacking; and business men would be relieved of much of the anxiety and worry that at times harass them under present conditions.

(4) The proposed plan would tend to pre-

vent those alternating periods of stimulation and depression of business known as "good times" and "bad times." It is not to be expected that any money system, however perfect, can wholly prevent excessive speculation, or development beyond the needs of the people, of particular industries; nor can it prevent such action from being followed by its natural consequences of disaster and loss. Wasted labour, like wasted force of any kind, can never be regained. Alternations of prosperity and adversity, of confidence and distrust, will probably always continue, as they always have; but much can be done to lessen the extent of the fluctuations. A money volume adjusted to keep prices constant, as a whole, will evidently operate to prevent prosperity from developing into a "boom" (sure to be followed by a more intense reaction), and will prevent the ensuing depression from reaching its extreme in panic.

(5) The adoption of the scheme would do no violence to existing business. It would

act rather as a mild stimulant by a slight raising of prices, and as a greater stimulant, through the confidence it would give. It would do no violence to the habits and customs of the people. Accustomed, as they already are, to a half dozen different kinds of paper money, the issue of a new one by the same authority to take the place of the others would hardly be noticed, especially as the change could be and ought to be made gradually.

If any change were necessary at a future time in the list of commodities constituting the standard, it could be made in the same manner that the standard was first fixed upon, with no disturbance of business, or perceptible change in money value.

(6) The interest received for such money would probably more than pay the interest on the outstanding government bonds, and would be as fair and equitable a form of taxation for that, or any other purpose, as could be devised.

(7) The coin and bullion we now use could be mostly shipped abroad in payment of our private debts, — represented by American securities held there, — and much interest money be saved to this country.

(8) Last, but not least, the plan would be a measure wholly American. This country would stand alone, free from the disturbing effects of foreign monetary legislation. Not that our foreign commerce would be lessened, or would be free from the effects of commercial disturbances in other countries: commerce is such a world-wide and intricate network that it would be impossible, even if it were desirable, for one country not to be affected by changes in others; but our money, the prices of commodities, as a whole, in that money, and the relations of debtor and creditor in this country would be free from foreign influences.

There are many minor merits in the plan, such as its tendency to equalize interest rates on the same, or on equally good, security all over the country; the facility with which money would flow from the central source to the point where it was needed, and return when not needed, instead of having to filter through many banks with much loss of time and expense, as it now does; the saving of what is now lost by abrasion of coin, etc.; but these points need not be enlarged upon.

Objections Answered.

It is to be expected that many objections would be raised to a plan, seemingly so radical as a whole, although it is in reality composed of old and tried methods in most of its parts. It may be well, therefore, to anticipate some of the objections likely to be brought forward and to endeavour to answer them.

Probably one of the first points to be raised against the plan, and one that, judging from recent discussion in magazine articles, would be strongly urged, is that it would have a bad effect on our foreign trade, and would divorce our prices from those of foreign countries.

It has already been shown, in the chapter on foreign commerce, that such fears are wholly unfounded, and that it makes no difference what the money is based on; if it is reasonably stable in value, foreign trade will not be disturbed.

In any event, ceasing to use gold in our domestic commerce would only leave a larger amount available for foreign commerce if it were needed. Gold would continue to be a commodity produced by this country, and dealt in as all commodities are, and if it were a necessity or convenience for the transaction of foreign business, the bankers engaged in such business would keep a sufficient amount on hand for their requirements. It is not believed, however, that any such necessity would be felt, either by the bankers doing a foreign business, or by the government in providing for the payment of interest on its bonded debt. The latter would probably have to be calculated in gold, in accordance with the terms of the contract, but could be paid as well in the current money. All such bonds would in a few years be redeemed, and any inconvenience from this source would be short-lived and slight at most.

As to divorcing our prices from those of other countries, the objection would have no weight. The *values* of any of our commodities, compared with those in other countries, would in no way be affected. No legislation can affect or determine the amount of one commodity that will exchange for another, either at home or abroad, except as it may alter the relations of supply and demand affecting them, by tariffs or taxes, or by the selection of some special one for a particular use, as is now done in the case of gold for money uses.

The values of gold, and of silver (to a less degree), would be the only things affected by the proposed change. All others would remain the same: the money of our own or any other country would continue to be used as a measure of such values, and if our prices rose as measured in such money, so also would foreign prices by the same measure. The exchange rates would vary as they now do, and between wider limits; but the variations would, probably, not be rapid enough to affect foreign trade injuriously. Our money would be constant in value, and if the gold varied, the slight inconvenience it might be to the few directly engaged in foreign trade would be a small matter compared with doing violence to our immense domestic commerce, by using such a variable standard.

In regard to all obligations that are made payable specifically in gold, they should, of course, be paid on that basis; but as the value of gold would be lessened by the shipment of it abroad, if we abandoned it as a money basis, the makers of such obligations would suffer less than they now do, or are likely to do in the future, because of the appreciation of gold value. Gold could always be had to meet such obligations by paying its current price, and that price would represent less of commodities in general than it now does.

It does not seem as if there could be any objection raised to the plan on the ground of unconstitutionality, since the greenbacks were, and are, held to be constitutional, and the new notes would be promises to pay gold and silver, as well as other commodities, if they were included in the list on which the money was based, not, to be sure, in a definite quantity, but in a definite value.

A more valid objection might be urged, in the danger of entrusting to public officials so great a power as the control of money value would seem to be.

In reply to this it may be said, that an inefficient, or to some extent even dishonest, control would be far preferable to no control at all, — which is the present condition. The greater concentration of capital in our modern industrial system, and the increasing values handled, necessitates the entrusting of greater responsibilities to individuals, in both public and private business, and it has not been found that the men selected for the higher positions of trust in public life were often recreant to the trust reposed in them, or inadequate to its responsibilities, even where much was left to their discretion. In the plan proposed, however, almost nothing would be left to the discretion of the officials in charge.

The act of Congress putting the plan in force could provide for any contingencies likely to arise, and the duties of the officials would be mandatory, so far as the adjustment of the volume of money was concerned and the method of accomplishing it. Beyond that, errors of judgment, or even of intention, could do little harm. Surely it is not expecting too much of a public official, that he shall carry out his mandatory instructions, especially as any variation therefrom would be liable to immediate detection, and could be corrected before harm was done.

It might be objected that the government

should not go into the banking business, that it is not one of its legitimate functions.

Avoiding the question of what the legitimate functions of government are,—about which there is room for a large difference of opinion,—it may be said that the plan does not contemplate the government entering the banking business as a competitor of existing banks, but rather as a regulator of them. This function it already exercises, and the popular demand is rather for an increase of such control. Furthermore, the Treasury, under the present system, is the largest holder of cash in the country, and its action is at any time of vital interest to the banks. It has more than once come to their aid in perilous times, to the extent of its ability, and had its ability been greater it could, and doubtless would, have done so more frequently. At times, moreover, the actual money held in the Treasury has been excessive, and by diminishing the volume of money in circulation this has badly affected business.

The proposed plan would prevent this, and while not materially enlarging the functions now exercised by the government, would make its control of the banking system more direct and effective, to the benefit alike of the banks and the public. Our present banking system, admittedly, shows much weakness in times of panic. Each bank expands its credits to the full limit in times of prosperity, for its own profit, and in time of distress contracts them for its own safety, thus increasing the distress at such times. Under this plan its safety, if solvent, would be assured without the need of contracting its credits.

As to controlling the volume of money, this either is, or is not, a proper governmental function. If it is, then justice demands that the control be efficient, and in the interests of an honest money. If it is not, — if the sole duty of government is to certify to the weight and fineness of pieces of metal by coining them, — then it has no right to refuse to coin any amount that may be presented of any metal the people or any section of them desire to use as money; no right to issue, or authorize others to issue, on government credit, any paper money; and no right to forbid, or prevent in any way, banks, firms, or individuals from issuing, on their own credit, any money they chose. All of these acts are a control of money volume. The mere statement of such an alternative is a sufficient refutation of the claim. It would simply be financial anarchy. The government must control money volume, and the control should be real, effective and honest.

Other objections might be raised to this plan, but none are foreseen of sufficient weight or gravity to offset in any considerable degree the merits it seems to present.

CHAPTER XI.

CONCLUSION.

A universal money for the whole world has been the dream of some writers. This in many respects would be a convenience, as would a general uniformity of weights and measures; but its benefits would be confined mainly to a saving of clerical work, and even this would not be as great an advantage as might be supposed, since differences in value of bills of exchange would continue to exist, even as they now exist between countries using the same money, or even between different cities of the same country.

Unless the universal money were stable in value, it would be as dishonest as the existing systems, and to make it stable would involve its absolute control in volume by some central power to which the various nations would delegate their authority. Such a thing is most unlikely to happen. The obstacles of national prejudice and habit are too strong to be overcome, — as will be evident from a perusal of Mr. Walter Bagehot's work, "Universal Money," — and the advantage to be gained by it is not worth the trouble. A universal money, then, must be considered as a Utopian dream; and a plan that provides for our own country an honest money seems to be the highest success to which we can at present aspire in the settlement of this vital and all-important question.

Whether future legislation be based on some such plan as the one here outlined, or whether another can be devised that will more closely meet the requirements, the fundamental principles we have considered should be kept in mind in any change that is made.

It should also be clearly understood that no monetary legislation, by this or any other country, can alter the relative values of all, or any, of the commodities, including gold and silver, which enter into human use and consumption, except in so far as such legislation shall affect their relative supply and demand. All that legislation can really beneficially do, is to provide a stable standard of value, as it now provides stable standards of length and weight, and to provide a medium of exchange that shall always conform in value to that standard, and shall be at once convenient and economical.

Opinions may honestly differ as to the best means of providing such a money, but, when fully understood, no difference of opinion can exist as to the benefit it would be to all classes of society, without exception.

The labourer gains by employment being more certain and constant; by the knowledge that open competition with capital will determine the shares of the joint product which each shall receive,— that he will not be the victim of an insidious change in money value or, while receiving nominally higher wages, be perhaps getting lower real wages. With an honest money, real and nominal wages coincide, and a rise or fall of wages is known at once as a benefit or an injury. The effect on wages would be toward an increase, by stimulating production and enhancing the demand for labour; while the labourer's ability to purchase more would absorb such increased production and improve his condition.

The employer of labour would gain by the certainty that his success will depend more largely on his own ability and endeavour, and less on causes which are not only beyond his control, but on which he cannot even calculate with certainty; while the greatest risks to which he is now subject will be removed.

This applies not only to manufacturers, but to industrial enterprises of all kinds.

Railroad stockholders would be especially benefited. No other business, perhaps, carries so large a fixed indebtedness, in proportion to its value, as railroads, and the stockholders suffer more from an advance in the value of money than most other owners. The fact that they are to some extent monopolies and can keep their rates the same, or even increase them, with money value rising, does not alter the case; for the amount of traffic will, under such conditions, be lessened, and it is impossible for most railroads to reduce expenses in anything like a proportion to the reduction of income from diminished business, because of the large fixed charges.

Merchants would be benefited by the greater general stability of prices, and would be relieved of many of the risks of business. They would, if solvent, have assurance that they could get money when needed, and the failures would be fewer.

Money loaners would also be benefited. It might seem, at first sight, as if they would not, since they profit directly by an increase of money value; but this is a narrow view.

While the money loaner, as before shown, gets an undue and unjust share of the products of labour and capital when prices are falling, yet the secondary effects of such a fall,—the increased competition for loans, and diminished demand for capital for business enterprises,—by lowering interest rates, tends to offset this gain; and the doubt and uncertainty as to security keep capital idle as well as labour. The lender gets a larger share of the total product than he is entitled to, under such conditions; but the total product is so much lessened as a whole, that his larger share is less in actual amount than a just share of the larger product would be, were money honest and prices constant. Moreover, one of the most important considerations to a lender is security, and this is much lessened with falling prices, and the loaner is frequently obliged to take the property which is security for his loan. He does not want the care and management of it, as it is generally far less valuable in his hands than in those of the original owner; the latter thereby loses something which he could use, and the former gains something he has no use for, and no one is really benefited. It cannot be considered, therefore, that loaners, as a class, either profit by or desire such a condition of business depression and panic as is largely produced by dishonest money.

A few individuals there may be — the leeches or wreckers of society — who rejoice at and profit by the general misfortune of all; but they are not, it is believed, sufficiently numerous to make their desires important or consideration for them a matter of anxiety.

In view of these considerations, the attempt — so often made in discussing the question of money — to set class against class, to lead labour to consider capital as its enemy, to embitter the relations between borrower and lender, and between the banks and the public, is greatly to be deplored. Competitors in a sense these different classes doubtless are, but so far as an honest money is concerned all are partners; all would be gainers by it and none losers. Past experience does not lead us to expect that men will generally become unselfish and altruistic in their motives in the near future. Business will continue to be, as it always has been, a struggle for the greatest amount of commodities with the least labour; and the plea for an honest money rests not upon altruism, but upon the enlightened selfishness which teaches that honesty is the best policy, in a money system as in other things, and that it is not profitable to kill the goose that lays the golden eggs.

INDEX.

Aldrich Report, the, 83.

Bagehot, Walter, quoted, 54, 122, 197.
Bank-notes, national, proposal for increasing issue of, 146.
Bi-metallism, 46, 67.
Böhm-Bawerk, von, quoted, 4, 7.

Capital and money, distinction between, 104.
Coin. *See* Money.
Coin and paper money, 22.
Cost of production, 10.
Credit, money forms of, 92.
Currency, an elastic. *See* Money.

Decline in prices, 90, 101.
Definition of money, 21.
Definition of value, 1.
Demand and supply. *See* Supply and Demand.
Dollar, gold and silver, 125.

Economist, London, on foreign prices, 83, 84, 86.
Ely, Prof. R. T., quoted, 32, 57.
Employers of labour, 102, 199.
Encyclopædia Britannica on money, 35.
Exchange, money as a medium of. *See* Money.

Existing monetary systems, 54.

Foreign commerce, 112-124; balance of trade, from an economic standpoint, a misnomer, 114; international trade, *ib*.
France, monetary system of, changed to a gold basis, 70.
Functions and requirements of money, 25.

Germany, monetary system of, changed to a gold basis, 70.
Gold. *See* Money and Monetary Systems.
Gold production between the years 1850-57 in Australia and California, 90.
Gold-standard arguments criticised, 98; Mr. D. A. Wells' fallacy of deeming labour a test of value, 100; threefold division of the community into labourers, employers of labour, and money loaners, 102; distinction between capital and money. *See* Stability of Gold and Silver Values.
Gold standard, the, 54.
Greenbacks, 126, 129, 146.
Gresham's law, 57, 59, 65, 67, 149.

INDEX

Inconvertible paper, 22, 76.
India, English commission on the depression of trade in, 119; silver currency in, 95.
Invariable money value, necessity for, 28, 40.

Jevons, Professor, quoted, 25, 27, 154.

Labour, productive and unproductive, 14; three kinds of, as factors in making for the value of a commodity, 15; labour not a standard of value, 18.
Laughlin, Prof. J. L., quoted, 46.

Medium of exchange, the, 164.
Mexican exchange, 120.
Mill, John Stuart, quoted, 6, 14, 18, 31, 36, 76.
Money loaners, 103, 200.
Money, definition of, 21; F. A. Walker's comprehensive definition, *ib.*; paper money and coin, 22 *sqq.*; functions and requirements of, 25; money as 'a medium of exchange,' 'a measure of value,' and 'a standard of deferred payments,' *ib.*; Professor Walker's substitution for the term 'measure of value,' 'common denominator of value,' 26; money as 'a store of value,' *ib.*; qualities necessary to a money material, 27; invariable value, 28; fluctuations in money value, 30; J. S. Mill on the purchasing power of money, 32; the *Encyclopædia Britannica* quoted, 35; money demand and supply, 36; money actual and money in forms of credit, 38; an invariable money value, 40; a change of money value, a robbery, 42; F. A. Walker, on decreasing money value, 44; a flexible or elastic currency, need of, 45; money in all countries a creature of the law, 53.
Money in the United States, 125; greenbacks, national bank-notes, silver and gold certificates, treasury notes, currency certificates, 126; gold coin, silver coin, 128; national bank-notes wrong in principle, 129; no means to-day of meeting either the increasing demand for money expanding population and commerce bring, or the sudden demand that a failure of credit may bring, 133; results, *ib.*; some proposed changes in our monetary system, 137; free coinage of silver, 138; erroneous views confuted, 139; 'greenback' or fiat money proposals, 146; increase of the issue of national bank-notes a mere makeshift, 147; divorce of our money from that of other countries only mode of controlling it and making it honest, 150; a new monetary system, 154; standard of value, 158; medium of exchange, 164; the national banks as a distributing agency, 167; complete control of the money volume, 177; merits of plan considered, 181; an invariable standard of value, *ib.*; a cheap, convenient, and elastic medium of exchange, *ib.*; prevention of panics, *ib.*; repression of excessive speculation and its reaction, 183, 184; plan wholly

INDEX. 207

American, 185; objections answered, 187; conclusion, 195.
Money system, our, some proposed changes in, 137.
Money value, 29.
Monetary systems, existing, 51; the gold standard, 54; Gresham's law, 57; the silver standard, 65; bi-metallism, 67; paper money, 71; J. S. Mill on inconvertible paper, 76.

New monetary system, a, 151–180.

Panics and hard times, causes of, 45; panic of 1857, collapse of credit in, 90; panic of 1873, 91.
Paper money, 71, 78; Prof. F. A. Walker on, 77. *See* Money.
Patten, Prof. Simon N., quoted, 7.
Prices, declining, evils of, 104; Professor Sherwood on stability of, 48.
Production, cost of, 10.
Purchasing power, 5.

Ricardo, David, quoted, 14, 17, 34, 46.

Sauerbeck, Mr., quoted, 83, 84, 87.
Sherwood, Sidney, quoted, 48.
Silver, *see* Money; the silver standard, *see* Monetary system.
Silver, free coinage of, 138, 139.
Silver famine of the Middle Ages, 82.
Silver production in Nevada, 91.
Silver standard, the, 65.
Silver-standard prices, 94.
Smith, Adam, referred to, 14.
Soetbeer, Dr. quoted, 83, 84, 87.
Stability of gold and silver values, 81–97; gold standard prices, 81; European economists on prices, 83; decline in prices, 90; silver-standard prices, 94.
Standard of value, the, 12, 158.
Supply and demand, 8; the immediate determiner of value the relation between supply and demand, *ib.*; the demand for a commodity determined by its subjective or exchange value, 9, 10; close connection between value and the ratio between demand and supply, 10.

Tauschkraft, 5.

United States, the, stops free coinage of silver, 70.
United States Senate Finance Committee Report on 'Wholesale Prices, Wages, and Transportations,' 83.

Value and the standard of value, 1–29; definition of value, 1; the two classifications — 'Value in use,' and 'Value in exchange,' 3; Böhm-Bawerk on 'Value in the subjective sense,' 4; John Stuart Mill's aphorism — 'every rise of value supposes a fall, and every fall a rise,' 7; Simon N. Patten on 'objective values,' *ib.*; standard of exchange value, 12; exchange value, what determines its constancy or variability, 19; only one real standard of value, 20.

Walker, Prof. F. A., quoted, 21, 24, 25, 77, 78, 82, 156.
Wells, David A., quoted, 70 *sqq.*; 94, 95, 98, 100, 104, 105–111, 119, 120.

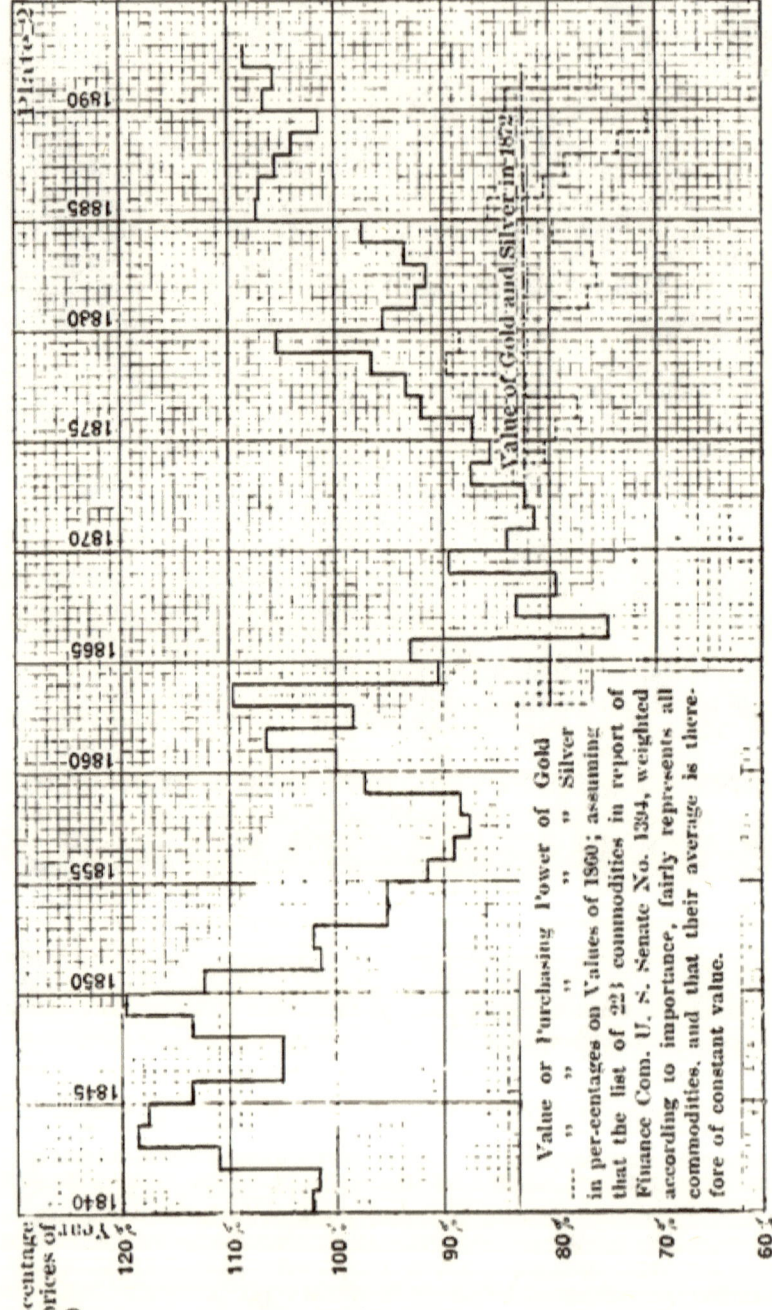

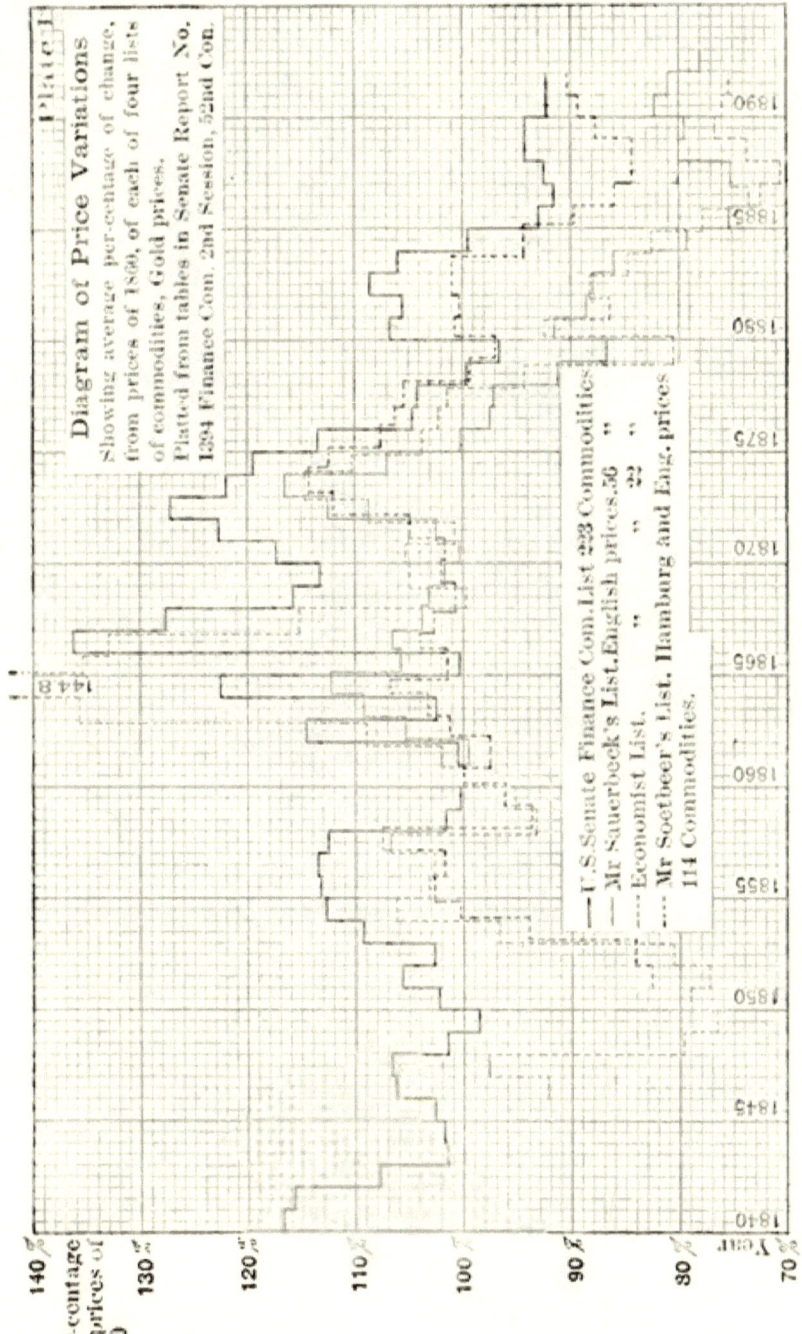

LABOUR

AND THE

POPULAR WELFARE.

BY

W. H. MALLOCK,

AUTHOR OF "IS LIFE WORTH LIVING?" "SOCIAL
EQUALITY," ETC.

Second Edition, 12mo, cloth, 90 cents.

"This new edition of Mr. W. H. Mallock's famous work, now published in a much cheaper form, will be heartily welcomed. The author's theories are his own, and his statements of fact may be relied upon as accurate. Few economic writers have compressed so much into so little space, and there is the advantage of clearness in brevity of statement. He writes earnestly. . . . It is no mean compliment to Mr. Mallock that his book is attacked by radicals and socialists on the one hand, and by conservatives on the other."— *Boston Daily Advertiser.*

"One cannot but recognize the earnestness of the writer, especially in the directions of making his book practical; and we are more deeply impressed with his words, perhaps, because he is in no way an extremist. He writes from the standpoint of a radical, not as an agitator, and he states his arguments and convictions forcibly and clearly."— *Detroit Free Press.*

"A sensible and practical work."— *Providence Journal.*

"The work is so carefully condensed as to be particularly practicable to the casual student of social questions, and also to those who have an awakening interest in the subject, without time or inclination for lengthy arguments."— *San Francisco Evening Post.*

MACMILLAN & CO.,
66 FIFTH AVENUE, NEW YORK.

THE
American Commonwealth.

By the Right Hon. JAMES BRYCE. D.C.L.,

AUTHOR OF "THE HOLY ROMAN EMPIRE," M.P. FOR ABERDEEN.

Third Edition, Revised Throughout.   In Two Volumes.
Large 12mo, $4.00, *net*.

This new edition has been practically rewritten, and not only have all difficult and controverted points been reconsidered, but in every possible way the information given is brought up to date. All statistics have been carefully corrected by the latest official records, and constitutional changes in the States since 1889 have been (so far as possible) noted.

Four entirely new chapters are added, in which the author discusses *The Tammany Ring in New York City*, *The Present and Future of the Negro*, *The South since the War*, and *The Home of the Nation*.

In the new material Mr. Bryce enters quite fully into recent politics, takes note of the issues of the last Presidential campaign, the effects of public opinion on such questions as the Force bill, the tariff, the silver question, in deciding the elections, the relations of the political parties to each of these topics, discusses at some length the growth of new parties, and comments on the Hawaiian troubles, new aspects of the agitation for female suffrage, etc.

The changes in the financial position of the Nation are commented upon, and the menacing attitude of Labor in recent years as shown in the Homestead Riots of 1892 and the Railroad Strikes in the present year. Attention is called to the dangers, on the one hand, of a constant influx every year of half a million of untrained Europeans, and on the other of the growing influence of wealth over the country, and such sinister results as "combines," huge corporations, etc., which are able to crush competition, and even influence legislation.

On the other hand, something is said hopefully of the efforts of municipal reformers to purify politics, and of the revolt of the better portion of the community in its effort to repress Rings, to minimize the action of the Machine, and overthrow the Rule of the Boss.

MACMILLAN & CO.,
66 FIFTH AVENUE, NEW YORK.

IN PREPARATION.

INDUSTRIAL COMBINATIONS AND COALITIONS

IN THE

UNITED STATES.

By ERNST VON HALLE.

12mo, cloth.

Dr. von Halle's work, on "Industrial Combinations and Coalitions in the United States," deals with an interesting and important subject. The scope of the work may be indicated by enumerating a few of the combines, in their broader sense, the author briefly touches upon, — such as the Standard Oil Trust, the Cordage Trust, Railway Pooling, Steamship Line Combines, Pork-Packing, Brewing and Distilling Combines, School Book, Wall Paper, and Playing Card Trusts, the Steel Trade Combine, the Western Union Telegraph System, General Electric Companies Trust, Express Service Combines, besides Gas and Water, and Postal Service, Copyrights, Patents, etc. The author's point of view is not controversial, but elucidatory and impartial, — seeking not to take sides for or against "Combines," still less to pass judgment upon them from a moral standpoint. He, of course, holds up to view their evils, — economical and political, — but, on the other hand, he points to their manifest industrial advantages. He shows how legislation has opposed them and sought to hold them in check, and he quotes both statutes and the decisions of jurists as repressive measures. Reference is also made to Trusts and their relation to the Stock market; while the subject is briefly considered as the outcome of a system of Protection. Here, as throughout, the author does not take sides, but contents himself, in the main, with a survey of facts. So neutral is the author, and averse from bias, that while he writes of monopolies as "despoilers, oppressors, and impoverishers," he at the same time commends them, as among the blessings of civilization, in giving encouragement to the invention and improvement of machinery and to the vast array of modern labor-saving processes which the age — even an age of combines and trusts — has produced.

MACMILLAN & CO.,
66 FIFTH AVENUE, NEW YORK.

THE UNITED STATES.

An Outline of Political History, 1492-1871.

By GOLDWIN SMITH, D.C.L.

12mo, cloth, $2.00.

"Considered as a literary composition, the work can scarcely be too highly praised. It is a marvel of condensation and lucidity. In no other book is the same field covered so succinctly and so well. . . . Almost every page is enriched with striking comments that cause the reader to carefully reconsider, if not to change, his views of many historical persons and events." — *The New York Sun.*

"The opinions advanced by Professor Smith are . . . in the main in harmony with those of our best authorities, and the treatise as a whole has a comprehensiveness of view and a ready grasp of leading tendencies that should make it particularly useful to the busy man who desires a rapid survey of American political history. By deliberately neglecting details Professor Smith has been able to fasten attention upon salient points and to concentrate interest around the careers of the great leaders in our political development. . . . It is safe to assert that Americans as well as Englishmen will welcome Professor Smith's book and rejoice in its noteworthy fairness and lucidity." — *The Beacon.*

"The history of the United States is now told for us in the more attractive form and with all the advantages of the marvellous power of condensation and the brilliance and picturesqueness of style which characterize Mr. Goldwin Smith's writing. The pages are filled with sentences which stimulate thought, with happy phrases, with vivid pictures of men and of situations drawn with a few bold strokes. . . . A volume of absorbing interest, worthy to be ranked with the best work of a great master of the English language." — *The Toronto Globe.*

"The author has, as those who know him do not need to be told, a style which is nothing less than fascinating, and a delightful literary flavor pervades all his work. The book is, of course, a marvel of condensation. Considered merely as a literary composition it would command high praise. Its lucidity, its graphic narration, and its constant avoidance of even an approach to dulness are quite as remarkable as its incisiveness of judgment and originality of view. . . . As a whole the book is remarkably free from errors." — *The Providence Sunday Journal.*

MACMILLAN & CO.,
66 FIFTH AVENUE, NEW YORK.

SOCIAL EVOLUTION.

By BENJAMIN KIDD.

NEW EDITION, REVISED. WITH A NEW PREFACE.

12mo, cloth, $1.50.

"The name of Mr. Benjamin Kidd, author of a very striking work on 'Social Evolution,' is, so far as we know, new to the literary world; but it is not often that a new and unknown writer makes his first appearance with a work so novel in conception, so fertile in suggestion, and on the whole so powerful in exposition as 'Social Evolution' appears to us to be, . . . a book which no serious thinker should neglect, and no reader can study without recognizing it as the work of a singularly penetrating and original mind." — *The Times* (London).

"It is a study of the whole development of humanity in a new light, and it is sustained and strong and fresh throughout. . . . It is a profound work which invites the attention of our ablest minds, and which will reward those who give it their careful and best thought. It marks out new lines of study, and is written in that calm and resolute tone which secures the confidence of the reader. It is undoubtedly the ablest book on social development that has been published for a long time." — *Boston Herald*.

"Those who wish to follow the Bishop of Durham's advice to his clergy — 'to think over the questions of socialism, to discuss them with one another reverently and patiently, but not to improvise hasty judgments' — will find a most admirable introduction in Mr. Kidd's book on social evolution. It is this because it not merely contains a comprehensive view of the very wide field of human progress, but is packed with suggestive thoughts for interpreting it aright. . . . We hope that the same clear and well-balanced judgment that has given us this helpful essay will not stay here, but give us further guidance as to the principles which ought to govern right thinking on this, the question of the day. We heartily commend this really valuable study to every student of the perplexing problems of socialism." — *The Churchman*.

MACMILLAN & CO.,
66 FIFTH AVENUE, NEW YORK.

www.ingramcontent.com/pod-product-compliance
Lightning Source LLC
Chambersburg PA
CBHW021834230426
43669CB00008B/967